Throwing the Bones

Jeannine Antoniou

Throwing the Bones – African Encounters
Beyond What can be Imagined
© 2013 by Jeannine Antoniou

Published in the United States by:

OLD STONE PUBLISHING

Old Stone Publishing
Boise, ID 83714
info@oldstonepublishing.com
First Edition
ISBN 13: 9781490309361
ISBN 10: 1490309365

Printed in the United States of America

Cover design by Laurel Profit
(www.clearwaterexpressions.com)

Cover leopard photo courtesy of
©Lukyslukys|Dreamstime.com

Unless otherwise noted, all photos are courtesy of
Jeannine Antoniou.

A portion of the proceeds of this book will go to Vulingquondo Creche, the South African preschool for:

Small Village Foundation
www.smallvillagefoundation.org

and

Mozambique Gorongosa
National Park Restoration
An African reserve in partnership with

The Greg Carr Foundation
www.gorongosa.org

and

Zoo Boise in Idaho

After 20 years in Africa, Jeannine wanted to share her barefoot experience with high school students by taking them to rural Africa. So she and her husband, Mark, formed the Small Village Foundation. In addition, Jeannine volunteers for Zoo Boise and is excited about their vision and partnership with Gorongosa Park in Mozambique, Africa.

Author's Note

Since childhood, my grandfather would challenge me, "Jump before you are ready," with arms open wide to catch me, "I will always be near." He was sixteen when he emigrated from Greece, leaving behind his home on a small island in the Aegean Sea. Inspired by wanderlust, curiosity, and the love of people in faraway lands, he is my Socrates.

This book is dedicated to the memory of my *grand* grandfather, Christos Antoniou, who died when I was sixteen.

T.S.S. Themistocles

For my children ~

Chris

Jen

Jamee

Kevin

Acknowledgements

It takes a village not only to raise a child, but to write my book.

Without the efforts of my editor/writing coach, *Jane Freund*, you would not be holding this book. Her patience and constant encouragement were with me every step on this lonely long journey. She believed in my stories, brought order to a riotous mass of memories and impressions that seemed hardly able to form a book. **Jane is my dream maker.**

At every high point and low point, my husband *Mark Smith* was my biggest fan, sometimes writing his own script in between mine. Often he was subjected to hearing paragraphs in excruciating detail with an incisive editor's eye, caustic wit and keen intelligence. He kept me fed and loved me through every rewrite. **He gave me restless wings and sturdy roots.**

For my children and family whose constant encouragement gave me hope. To my sons: *Chris*, who has been with me since the beginning, **you inspire me.** *Kevin*, whose Greek DNA spills into his own writing, I appreciate your challenge "to slay the dragons, without fear of what others may think." **You are my example**. My daughters: *Jamee*, who has walked her own "dark path of Africa," **you teach me humility**. *Jen*, who never gave up on herself or on her mother, **you amaze me with your understanding**.

It is surprising writers have any friends as the last chapter comes to an end. **Dear friends, you have been there, challenging me to write honestly, sharing with me what I need to hear.** Thank you, Dee, Betsy, Elizabeth F. For my out-of-the-ordinary-Mormon friends, Arlea, Liz Joan, Jan J., I am grateful. Kevin L., Amy S., Molly H., Melissa N., Jan T., the many friends through Small Village Foundation, South African acquaintances, Dr. Diana Russell, Wendy DeLa Harpe, Tema, Zanani Mandela, Ela Gandhi, Sindiwe Magona, author of *Mother to Mother*, in Soweto Shoki and Bheki, in Wyoming: Toni and Laurel and the Wyoming Writers Group.

Other gifted professionals: Laurel Profit/Book Cover, Julie Rember/Copy Editing, Dan Sullivan/Publisher and guru of formatting, Melissa Nodzu original Leopard Design/Marketing, Thom Hollis/Graphic Design, my first editor Elizabeth Lyon, Dr. Katey Coffing, Dr. Patricia Ross and Kate Riley, Natalie Goldberg, author of *Writing Down the Bones*, the only book I took with me to Africa.

Volt author *Alan Heathcock* was my teacher in the Fiction Writing Class at Boise State University: I acknowledge your talent as **a teacher who knows how to take the student to the deepest places and write truthfully.** He recently penned on his Facebook page:

"As the helpless feeling lingers, I'm out in my trailer using all the sadness and anger to write something that matters. It's not all I can do to change the world, but it's what I can do today, and it's what I do best. I believe a story told true and written well is about as powerful a weapon as can be wielded against injustice and human suffering."

Encounters

Prologue
Swaziland, South Africa

Leopard
Apartheid - My Story

Dance of the Witchdoctor
Sangoma
The King's Royal Hunt
Cowgirl

Kipengee
Voices Clairaudient
Secrets Trapped

Mamba
The Bushveld Code
"Siyinquba"
Shadow of Death
Ritual in Sand and Ceremony
National Geographic

Disappointment

Polish Priest Meets Mormon Infidel
Praying Mantis
I Needed Africa More Than it Needed Me
No Stranger to Death
Zulu Mother
Orchids and Prayers

The Day I Was no Lady

"Do your little bit of good where you are; it's those little bits of good put together that overwhelm the world."

~Bishop Desmond Tutu

"... this path of Africa exudes a will of its own. Cradled in unknown innocence, the traveler is beguiled by an untamed beauty. The heart kneels in the twists and turns of the wind dusted roads of red."

~Ernest Hemingway

Prologue
1989

The goal of our journey, our quest,
is to penetrate the mystery of life's events.
African oral tradition

The stories you are about to read are a collection of essays spanning two decades that chronicle an unlikely journey into the unknown. I had come to live on the southern tip of the African Continent, where seasons reverse, sunsets defy the sky, nothing is familiar, and reality shakes you at the core. It was another path. Another land, near the birthplace of mankind, many believed.

Swaziland, a small independent country, had retained its ancient traditions. It did not survive Britain's colonial stronghold, but has been vigilant in withstanding modern ways besieging its borders.

I did not know where this uncharted, bone-crossed path would lead. I was going to test my depth of trust and intuition I had gained in the last few years. Always excited about the unknown and unexpected adventure, I found the answers to be not as important as the questions. It did not matter what I would face along the way, I would figure it out. I wanted to know the person I thought I had become.

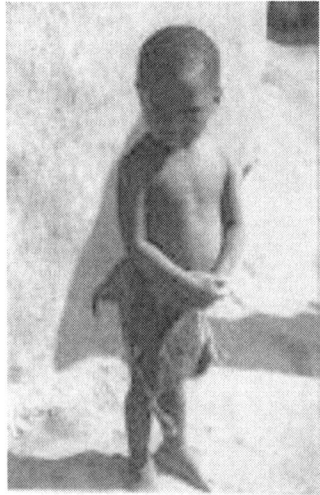

There were many considerations in choosing Swaziland. Perhaps it was the raw enchantment of living in one of the last remaining African kingdoms. This was a place where everyone belonged based on the blood of their ancestors. It was where a child still plays in a loincloth of animal skins and runs barefoot in the village, kept safe by his many mothers.

I remember researching before I came the first time in 1989. I was fascinated by these people of Zulu descent, who migrated down from the north. I wondered why there was little detail written in their history books. I have never understood why I was drawn to this ancient culture. In that year of preparation, I struggled for any signs of logic, especially when friends would ask why I was going to Africa. Strangely, it felt the decision was made without me. I had to only come to terms with a few questions.

How was I going to be bold enough to explain that I was leaving to my conservative boss, who thought all African Americans should be shipped back to Africa? What about the truest of friends, who stood by me during the separation from my husband, and who avoided the gossip of a devastating divorce, would they think I was running away?

Was I running away?

If I was going to find meaning in my life, I had to leave. There was no other recourse. The time had come to talk to my family; if I waited any longer I would only look more foolish. The airline ticket was purchased. One suitcase packed. My 30-day notice submitted.

I had set up a time to talk. Emotions were on end. I felt unstrung and spiritless. All the reasons I wanted to go seemed selfish now. I suddenly needed permission like a child. Something was holding me back, as if a cold hand had grabbed me by the back of my neck.

"Soon I will be going to live in Africa." My oldest son, Chris looked at me with his father's eyes.

"This is crazy, Mom." His tone lowered. I fought back the tears.

"What about your three grandchildren? They won't know who you are." I was afraid to admit that I didn't know who I was.

I listened in silence to his reasoning, almost wishing he would talk me out of leaving. He walked away shaking his head.

It was crushing to leave him disappointed. This subject was never discussed again, nor did I discuss subsequent visits to South Africa. Still in their young adult years, my children would not understand the global implications of a country oceans away deep in the throes of apartheid, a word unfamiliar to them, and most of the world.

In their innocent minds, there would be no justification if they knew how their mother had become impassioned with the prison release of Nelson Mandela. How could I hope they would understand my afternoon with the granddaughter of Gandhi in her office of the African National Congress?

I asked myself, how could they know that in the protected bubble of the Mormon world I raised them in, only babies during the civil rights movement? In the middle of my changing diapers of two little boys, they did not see me in the stupor of disbelief when President Kennedy was assassinated. They were too young to know how a country deeply mourned the killing of Dr. Martin Luther King, Jr.

The year was 1963; motherhood was foremost in my mind. I buried unsettling questions in the face of tumultuous changes surrounding the nation. I was taught to never challenge the U.S. government's absolute authority. The unpopular demonstrations against Nixon's Vietnam War swirled in the back my mind.

However, most frightening was the creeping doubt of my religiously structured foundation. Because of the Mormon immoveable stand on racial issues, my devotion was severed.

Several years later, our family felt complete with the birth of two delightful daughters. Life seemed normal on the surface. The love of my children was enough. In the busy day-to-day activities, I lived in a convoluted world, escaping conflict, controversy and reality. Years passed, before I was able to come to terms with my failing marriage, and a church demanding my silence of how sacred vows were shattered.

Swaziland, South Africa

There is always something in the self that is either over-compensating, pretending, giving in, or pushing too hard. The only way one can reach to move it out is through ritual.
Sobonfu Some

The rhythmic sounds of the drums in the Swazi heartland kept me a willing prisoner for a year. This was a unique culture, embedded in long-held customs, and was a safe place for me. In the unspoiled wilderness of Mkhaya Game Reserve, I would run my three miles beside zebra herds twice a week.

The full August moon was slowly rising in a place most of the world would never see. I was an invited guest to a land many call "the only jewel of Africa, where the spirit of oneness and belonging abides."

I was fascinated by the young King Emswati (seen on the left in this picture). He was struggling to keep peace in his monarchy, since the passing of a sixty-year reign of his father, King Sobhuza II. He was often caught between the traditions of his people, and a world of new ideas encroaching their borders.

5

In the many days of silence to follow my time in this small kingdom, I saw glimpses of how pieces of life could fit together. However, I was still unwilling to surrender a protected heart, like the high fenced walls of the king's kraal, surrounding his prized cattle, impenetrable.

Living in a mud hut does not make one primitive.

Leopard

Leopard

The mournful cry of the leopard was a sound of comfort for Mahaya. She remembers watching from a distance, the fierce strength in the leopardess and her cubs. "There is an ancient intertwining; we learned to dance around each other."

I listened to Mahaya, the youngest wife of her husband. Shy. Careful. Like the leopard, she lives with people but goes unnoticed.

"The good smell of the village, the smell of heat, wild dogs, unkempt gardens, and people." It was easy for me to romanticize in the clicking sounds of her Zulu language.

"...all put together, was the smell of what was life."

Leopards became Mahaya's animal symbol of muti magic, the black powder in a small bottle. It enabled her to see what the leopard sees when all appears dark, adapt to change during hard times, and draw on the instinct to survive.

I was mesmerized in her story of the leopard. The village women taught her how the leopard intuitively trusts, without answers.

She whispered to me—
"Know who you are. Be still...quiet fills the future of unexpected goodness."

Thando Mahaya had to learn quickly from her husband's wives. Every year they were given a small plot of land to farm, to tend and to guard. Life was simple. Few decisions were left for the youngest wife.

Her story paused. I waited. The mud walled home was dark, except for the flickering candle. Her deeply set eyes looked away. "Some seasons, our village would wake to the ground shaking and see the aftermath of raging elephants. Ripened maize was left to die in the red clouds of dust. Hope disappeared in the unmet cries of hunger and our children's swollen bellies."

A blanket of grey smoke smothered the small coal fire. Near the entrance to the hut, I watched the broken pieces of bleached straw float down on beds of heat waves. Outside, I could hear the echo of Mahaya's words, as wild dogs became scavengers in the unkempt gardens.

Apartheid – My Story

This is Africa. Ordinary life springs above a bitter path to find the resilience of another day. Their journey becomes my journey. In refuge, I escape from a suffocating heat to cooled huts of mud. I listen to stories of the Bushman, the Xhosa, and the Swazi King with countless wives who truly understood how to live in peace.

Like the worn edges of my passport, I turn the page from one culture into another. In the end, I rediscover my own.

Always welcome, I was an outsider on the frayed edges of apartheid. Haunted by unjust decisions for heroes of The Struggle, I stumbled to keep in step beside the proud South African, both of us on the road of reconciliation.

Once home, I saw my own apartheid, the separateness I created, of prejudice in preconceived shadows. I felt the dignity of ancestors; I was born of Greek and Swedish immigrants; raised from the loins of Mormon pioneers.

In time, I would find love in the most unexpected place. I kept a tiny bottle of muti magic tucked in my leopard pajamas folded in a drawer near my bed. At night there were times I could not sleep thinking about one of the last things my mother said to me, "… remember Jeannine, you come from a long line of lusty women."

I write my story because I have lived my story.

Dance of the Witchdoctor

Sangoma

The traditional healer, with his own story to tell, is honored in the village. My Sangoma experiences remain unexplained.

Curious and excited, I was eager to meet my first healer; Sandile Hlope had been assigned by the ancestors of his tribe to be my clairaudient guardian. He was to teach me the art of hearing the unspoken from the earth that gives power to words. Somehow, he knew I was in preparation for a dry desert voyage in the days and months to come. Sandile would be waiting for me, "beside the river with no water."

I stumbled down a steep slope. Barely missing the stinging nettle, I launched into the hidden weaponry of a thorn tree. My arm throbbed. I dismissed the bright blood seeping through my sleeve. I was late. Over the rough boulders, his patriarchal silhouette was shadowed against the evening sky. A wool red and black traditional blanket was draped around his shoulders.

"Most important" his first words, "everything has a soul, this rock, even that tree by the river with no water."

He was a teacher of all things Swazi. My mind swayed back and forth from the strange pull of his old world ways. He began to weave the story of a ceremony about the young man who comes to the spring hunt "which happens only in the fullness of the moon."

"My words spring up from the bones of the ancestors." A soft chant began, "I raise my hand in trust to the religion of my tribe. Praise God for the blood of the bull which brings strength to our loins, and for the milk of the cow which gives warmth to the breasts of our lovers."

This scene was far from *Romancing the Stone*, I thought.

Sandile pulled a dry gourd to his thick brown lips and "drank the milk" of his religion. My stomach rumbled with the smell of the rancid milk, curdled for days in the clotted red blood. Nauseous, I swallowed hard and held my breath. Hopefully he wouldn't make me drink from the gourd to test my understanding in the ways of the Sangoma. I was ready for his clairvoyant ancestors to give up on me.

The moonlight caught the shiny edge of my guardian's sword. It was as much a part of him as the sinews of his body. Sandile ignored my face faded in color and confidence. He probably didn't know what to do with this white woman, cloistered behind modern-day prophets, and so-called western sophistication.

He continued, "This spear is a manifestation of my faith, without it I can achieve nothing, no land, no cattle, and no wives." I imagined him in an earlier time, his face young and muscled body hard standing before his tribe. "Honor will be mine, after my circumcision. I will survive in the bush for thirty days. Like the seeds of wild grass my village will come to witness my allegiance to them. This spear is the emblem of my blood and breeding."

I was impressed by this boyhood ritual. The love for the beauty and usefulness of his spear was inspiring, a symbol of his manhood.

We began walking toward his village. The night was black; I could almost reach the stars that had come so close to us. Our pace quickened.

"Tonight, I want you to learn about another world, the world of the Sangoma. I am blessed by the knowingness of the Sangomas. These spiritual healers know what life is for and how it is to be lived as they throw the bones," the strength in Sandile's voice assured me.

"Throwing the bones is a clear manifestation of how pieces of the journey fit together in balance. The bones, crushed roots and shells speak of our connection and will fall as destiny guides them to scatter to the red earth of Africa."

I was beginning to see my own humanity reflected in the humanity of these Swazi people. I was called sister, mother, or grandmother, never by name. Each day I learned important life lessons. For example, the old king wanted his people to know the language of their neighbor. He had many wives, many from other countries; it was his way toward lasting peace.

One of his favorite sayings was, "remember, no man is greater than any other man." I thought how this simple philosophy of King Sobhuza II could keep wars from even starting.

The evening was just beginning its adventure. I followed in Sandile's footsteps, this man, a man because of his spear. He was honored by his ancestors, and by me. The lights from the fires of his village made a safe refuge.

A woman's strange dramatic cry rose above the beating drums. I didn't know the path I was on with Sandile. But I did know in split seconds Africa could be as ruthless as any sea. I walked closer to him. He smiled.

The air carried the smell of lingering smoke from the coal fires. My eyes burned. I could only see shadows of graceful moving bodies dancing in unison.

I didn't notice when Sandile disappeared.

Cowhide skirts rustled. Around their soft brown shoulders, draped beadwork delicately attached to an animal skin modestly covering the married women. This could have been a scene from the book, *Out of Africa*, primordial paragraphs written by Isak Dinesen, the Swedish born author, who never lost the longing for her beloved Africa, a place she called the cradle of mysteries.

In the protective circle women came from every direction. Some danced reaching up into the sky like shooting stars on a barefoot path near the edge of the escarpment.

When the morning came, I could see the veld stretch to the western border, between the granite mountains, where rivers tumbled through deep gorges. It was time to find my way home.

Not far from the horizon of rounded thatched huts, I came into a clearing surrounded by tall grass, where elephant, rhino and lion once met brave warriors in leopard skins, running fast behind their spears of manhood.

The King's Royal Hunt

I was invited into the inner circle of an ancient tradition. An untamed scene was about to unfold. The king had planned the annual Royal Hunt in the shadow of his father's grave near the Mountain of Buried Kings (as pictured above).

We walked toward the village, beneath the sheltering sky, watching the horizon fade into a mysterious blood orange light reflecting on the mountain, lifeless, alone in the distance. The smoke curled above the thatched huts, the smell of burning coal drifted through the warm night.

Excitement scattered among us as we sat on the hand-carved pine wood benches. I had not noticed I was the only woman. A large fire ignited into the backdrop of the sky. Drums beating, I could feel the earth move beneath me as a hundred warriors began to dance. Their Swazi shields made of leather hid the leopard loincloth around their hips. The dry African dirt plumed up like red smoke around their feet. I could not take my eyes off their bare bronze chests. Their muscles synchronized in sensual rhythm, they jumped high into the air and came down to the ground in pounding unison.

Mesmerized in the seduction of undulating bodies, I was unaware of the lean young warrior coming toward me. He held his shield up above his head. The men chanting in the background stopped. Suddenly he threw his shield down at my feet. I thought this must be a sign of bravery, not knowing what to do in the middle of Africa, I stood to thank him. It would be two days later I would find out the meaning of this great display of valor. The men left for the hunt into the pine forests near the sacred burial place where all the kings lay to rest.

Cowgirl

Several days later, the young king sent one of his military defense forces to visit me. In the doorway the regent stood tall, regal, a diagonal red sash over his bare shoulders. Brown, like chocolate before it melts, his body met my eyes. I could hardly think, when I noticed only a leopard skin below his waist.

Between masculinity and a hidden mischievous smile, he remained serious in the call of duty. Without flinching, his black eyes focused straight above my head. He handed me a formal letter, the King's royal stamp affixed on the back. In wild expectation, I could not imagine what he wanted. One of his uncles, a prince who looked like he could have been the older brother of Denzel Washington, had formally asked me to be his 14th wife.

Taken aback, I gave him my biggest non-Swazi smile and thanked him. With a gracious bow, lower than usual, out of respect for his uncle, I said I would speak to the head of the household where I was living.

Before I finished my short response, he interrupted to say his uncle was prepared to offer more than he had ever given before, *a bride price of two hundred cows.* Honored and amazed, I thanked him again and he left.

"*No*" was not an acceptable answer, I was told by my Swazi family. They continued to explain about the night of the Royal Hunt, the young warrior was the bearer of this marriage request when he threw his shield down at my feet. Everyone knew but me.

I was a great-great-granddaughter of a polygamist Mormon family that helped to settle Utah. This being one of many wives was not a foreign idea.

Throughout the next week, I heard stories of many unmarried women who had barely escaped being kidnapped by the Royal Family.

But two hundred cows at $1,000 each, I mused, was an interesting thought.

Kipengee

"Kipengee"

Summer 1990

I was a woman near my 48th birthday, a woman in the middle of a love affair with the land and with the self I met in Africa.

I wanted to be free from the voices of the past. For seven months, I tested the limits of my emotional endurance. Each day I grappled with loneliness too bitter to taste. The heartache of leaving home a mother, no longer a wife, and a Mormon Infidel became a part of the landscape I walked.

Never did I envision a path that would take me to Africa, certainly not a place where most Mormon grandmothers would ever go.

Another dry day in Swaziland, I wanted to say aloud. I climbed the last hill toward the school, thinking of my daughter living with her father's new wife. I held back the tears, stopped feeling sorry for myself, and remembered *the last thing Africa needs is my tears.* Even their babies do not cry.

It has been written that this was once the land of the Bushman, a place where distance and death does not end relationship. The burning pain in my legs was a good distraction from the pain of missing family.

I looked around at the vast valley below and took in a deep breath. As a soft wind swept through the golden veld, I breathed in the air, the air of Eden.

The Bushman understood his past and his destiny. What he left behind on rocks and caves was his story in art, of words without an alphabet. I wondered what the word he used for *paintbrush*, this artist who spoke in a language of clicks.

Unlike the Bushman who knew his destiny, I was in search for mine in Africa.

I trekked the Bushveld three miles each day to teach at a school. During an earlier visit to this remote village, the Headmaster had shown me a tattered manual, the front cover worn off, pages faded and corners curled. "The History of South Africa" was written by an Englishman from Johannesburg. Without warning, the enthusiastic Headmaster called for his people to gather. "Like the story of Jonah and the whale...the Lord has given us this woman to help our young students." He heaved the book into my arms and made me a teacher.

In the thatched schoolhouse made of mud, I was the shortest in a room full of children of all ages and only boys. Each day I held the heavy book and stumbled through the names of old kings, ancient rivers and mystical rituals. They laughed with me in my attempt to make the clicking sounds of their language. I soon learned these rowdy young warriors already knew their history, and lived the traditions passed down from their fathers.

Voices Clairaudient

On the way to school, I brushed aside the tall grass of Swaziland and dared not to think of anything slithering or coiled to strike. It is said the mamba has a distinct scent of curry. *A prudent clue*, I mused while surveying the ground ahead of me.

Someone came running toward me from the village. *"Kipengee, kipengee"* a young man shouted in his clicking SiSwati language.

"Take the detour our children walk," his father rushed over to translate, *"when you take a short cut,"* he pointed to a nearby moun-

tain, *"your walk is half."* I knew the mountain pass through the royal burial ground of the Swazi Kings was forbidden.

I should have known not to go without official permission out of respect for their ancestors.

The path ended at the edge of an embankment eroding into a shallow stream. My sandals came off; I hiked up my skirt and jumped across the Giardia-infested water. Like the children, I continued barefoot.

Not far from the mountain, I ignored the gut premonition and the sudden chill. I felt very vulnerable, and walked faster. It was then that I sensed a strange stirring beneath me. In the earth-hardened catacombs, a pulse of clairaudient voices began to flow up through my feet.

I shivered and struggled to separate the eerie words from my own.

Fragments of sanity escaped, when the echo of voices grew louder, *"Write the story."* My body froze in the frightening slow motion of a bad dream. Coming to my senses, I could not understand what had just happened. Desperate to disprove the experience, I retraced my steps with sandals on.

Within moments, the mysterious voices pleaded, *"Write the story."* This time I heard, not with ears, but from every nerve in the souls of my feet.

This was an unbelievable story. I vowed never to tell anyone.

Stunned and confused, I sat down on the flat edge of a rock to gather my composure. I reached for the small notebook I carried and penciled, *Write ... write the story.*

Each day I wrote – how I heard the laughing voices of children from a distant village; and how I watched an early morning sky of crystalline blue folding itself around the hills, around the mother who does not cry. I remembered the voices of Mormon grandmothers who pushed handcarts with babies and belongings into a "promised land" – and the brave smile from my daughter the last time I saw her.

Secrets Trapped

June 2011

"They call me Dinosaur Tracker." Dr. Dan reached down and shook my hand. His grip was strong, and like many South African men was ready for adventure. He was born in South Africa, but lived in Canada. When not saving lives as a physician, he was a part-time archeologist.

In June 2011, Dan was invited to an excavation site and invited me with him to visit the place where archaeologists were digging at a site in South Africa. A trove of sophisticated stone tools had been discovered. The scientists believed they were made 50,000 years before the technology to create them emerged in Europe. This finding, reported in the journal "Nature," could mean the first modern humans evolved where the Indian Ocean meets the Atlantic.

We arrived at the dig near the southernmost tip of the continent; an excited Dr. Dan was ahead of me bounding over rocks. He talked about another dig in the 1880s where artifacts of the Bushmen known as Khoi-San were discovered close to his boyhood home.

"Early dwellers lived on a diet of shellfish and tubers rich in protein and energy," claimed Dr, Dan, "so eat your veggies," he called out over his shoulder. When we reached the cave there were students everywhere. Some focused on screening soil samples, others numbering earth fragments of early human life.

A year later it would be reported, "...the findings were of incredible significance, not only for South Africa, but for Africa and the world."

Deep in the cave, brackish water dripped into dank decay, the ancient smell of secrets trapped. Centuries of layered earth told a story of existence and extinction. The director talked of "the cultural importance, and structures situated at the largest project of its kind in the world today."

It was cold and damp on the narrow ledge. Away from the group, I listened to the echo of the academic detailed lecture. My body ached as I stood for several hours trying to imagine the life lived over 150,000 years ago.

"...and there are many unmarked burial sites here," the director pointed to the back of the cave. He had my immediate attention. My mind flashed back to the voices I had heard twenty years earlier. I wondered how the First World archeologist would respond.

Late in the afternoon, iridescent lights were unplugged and laptops closed. Outside the waves threw themselves over the path covering the final footprints of Dr. Dan, the dinosaur tracker.

The director came out from the cave and walked over beside me. For the first time he looked at me. I could not escape the edge of the cliff. I did not know what to do with myself or even where to look.

Words jammed in my throat. Like the voices I heard that day from the earth-hardened catacombs, my submissive voice had been under the patriarchal order of religion.

In the southern hemisphere, the fast descent of the sun leaves only a few moments of twilight. Eclipsed by time, I blurted out my hidden question.

"In your years of excavating in Africa, have you ever *thought* you heard voices coming from the earth?"

My eyes burned. Words froze in the space between us. He looked down; his feet unbalanced on the jagged rocks, and retreated back into nowhere.

I began to thank the man of science for his time, but he interrupted. "Yes, I have heard voices… The first time I dismissed it. When it happened again…academic fences collapsed.

"I did not understand, but believed it was important to document. What I did know…this experience was best never to talk about."

There may have been more words pass between us, but none were needed as we walked up the path. I felt exonerated from the memories of self-doubt.

The pounding surf crashed behind me. I turned around one more time to see the blue in two colliding currents of the Indian and Atlantic, magically held there as if by a spell.

"Writing a book is a lonely thing. like crying with all your heart into the night, when there is no-body to hear you cry ~ nobody to answer you."

~Wilber Smith
South African author

Mamba

Mamba

Simon Mdawe lay motionless on the bare army cot in a makeshift village clinic. Barely breathing, he was comatose, while his family pressed close with murmurs of sobs and prayers. His ankle was swollen with two small puncture marks appearing in the middle of an ever-growing purple bruise. The venom's effect would be fatal. Simon Mdawe would be dead within an hour.

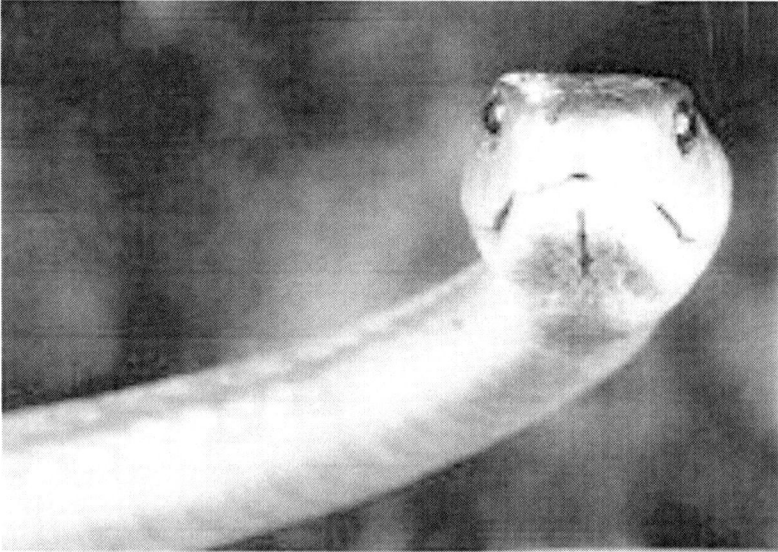

One of the most fearsome snakes in southern Africa, the mamba can be seen slithering over rocky slopes, coiled in a tree hiding, or nestled deep in a termite mound. Black mambas kill over 20,000 people a year.

Compared to other snakes such as the phlegmatic puff adder, the mamba is well camouflaged and little inclined to avoid approaching footfalls. Drop by drop, the Cape cobra's venom even outpunches the mamba, as does that of the southern African boomslang. However as a total package, the black mamba has no peer in its realm; even the dead snake's fangs are as fatal as a live bite.

I had every reason to be afraid every day, every step, even in that imagined empty place in the air where it could have been. I vowed if I ever encountered its coffin-shaped head and humorless smile, I would be forever "out of Africa."

The Bushveld Code

"That bloody snake can be as long as eight feet," said Oom Terblanche, an Afrikaans farmer from the Tshwane region near Botswana. "Their mouths are inky black when threatened and their cardio-toxin venom can kill a dozen men within an hour." I had been duly warned by Oom, who towered above me and lived by the Bushveld Code (always carry a gun). His hat bristled with guinea-fowl feathers and his lips curved into an exuberant smile that hid in his red rough beard.

We walked around to the front of his Dutch Colonial farmhouse standing as it had always stood for over a hundred years. In deep thought, he looked out on the fertile land.

"This is the legacy of my ancestors the Voortrekkers who came from Holland," he said, pausing long enough to remember how to translate his mamba horror story from Afrikaans to English. "Would you like a cup of tea, Rooibush tea, with sweetened milk?"

On the stoop of his veranda we were shaded by long vines of magenta bougainvillea.

"With only a few hours of daylight left, I hurried to finish plowing with my tractor. I was concentrating on the furrow in front of me." His voice lowered. "Nearly done, I stopped suddenly when I felt a dark shadow behind me. Shivers raced down my body, standing my hair on end at the back of my neck. Slowly I turned around to see what was behind me. Just at the back of the tractor, the meanest black mamba I had ever seen was standing on its tail. Little Missy, he was high as I was tall even sitting on the seat of my tractor."

With each bigger and braver story told of a human's last-minute escape or the mamba's final execution, one thing I knew for sure: Africa is never dull. Even though I was terrified of someday seeing a mamba wound around a tree, with its nape flared like a cobra, I would not admit a slow growing fascination and respect.

"Siyinquba"

One late afternoon when the honeyed sunlight descended behind Swaziland's great Mariepskop Mountains, Menzie, a young Swazi boy, and I were finishing a walk down a small hill of rock crannies, pocked with deep holes. It was impossible to miss stepping on some of the dark openings.

"Could there be black mambas in these holes?" I dared question.

"But of course, Mkulu." He called me his grand grand-mother, the African equivalent of grandmother. "This is their home."

I was the intruder. Regardless of my fear, I had to be re-minded of this lesson many times. Menzie's family loved to share innumerable stories of Swaziland's "old king," His Majesty King Sobhuza II who reigned beginning in 1921. To him, all life was precious; snakes should be preserved, not wantonly destroyed. "Nature balances itself," he admonished his people. "What right do we have to kill a creature who is going its way? Snakes help kill rats and mice. They could be manifestations of the ancestors, so we must be the sanctuary. Our motto is 'Siyinquba' – we are their fortress. They could be a sign of our royal ancestors." Over fifty years later, the Swazi nation still believed in the legends of wisdom of the "old king."

Shadow of Death

"African problems must be solved by African ways," the old king's ways reassured me too. In time, there would be a solution to wild imaginings of walking alone, when without warning I would feel a throbbing sharp bite only to look down at blood dripping from a black mamba's venomous strike. Its fangs still holding on to my flesh, I would know that I only have moments to live once the pure neurotoxins enter my body.

First a bad taste like metal would come in my mouth. It would be hard to breathe; my lips numb; a sense of lightness. Soon a warm feeling would overtake my body. I would pass into a coma-like state and be taken for dead, wondering when my family back home would be notified.

It is part of the cultural folklore, tales of survival I wished I had never heard.

The fear of fear raises its head, constantly taunting me. Old people in the village call the snake the "shadow of death." However, they also tell me there is a cure; it would take only a visit with the Head Traditional Healer, a Sangoma, and his promise in the magic of muthi blessed by honored ancestors. The Africans take comfort in magic; it is a power intrinsically neutral, neither good nor evil, something to utilize. At this point, I was ready for anything; even a lofty promise by a witchdoctor. Curiosity rarely kept me from an adventure.

The ritual would begin when the moon is full to allow the bright beacon of wisdom to shine through. The day arrived. Later, when the first star was seen, a selected few men and their wives accompanied me to a sacred circle where a fire was burning. The women stayed on the outside. Menzie sat close beside me propping up my courage.

With no easy exit, I sat in the middle of these self-appointed Swazi warriors whose words ruled the hut, the village, their kingdom, and me, tonight. The sweat began to drip down my chest. Holding my breath, I could have never guessed what would come next. Menzie whispered, "sometimes the wind will tell a story." I listened to the night noise.

The fire crackled, spitting a fang-like spark surely aimed at me. I looked up, hoping no one saw me jump. However, everyone's attention was focused on the swaying flames of the fire. I heard the ground crunching under heavy footsteps coming toward us. Surprised no one turned around, I was certain they all knew something I did not. My muscles froze and would not move. It was like being a hostage tied up in a bad dream.

In an instant, the circle was broken. From out of the darkness, I glanced to see only the frame of a shaman-looking man with feathers tied in a spotted leopard headband. Afraid to see his face, my attention was fixated on his feet and the dusty sandals dyed red by the Swazi soil. He walked with a long powerful stride and carried a carved fighting stick. Dried goatskin stripes were fastened around his ankles, and the rustle of attached rattles broke the dark silence.

Tufts of cow tail hung below his knees switched back and forth and flickered in the dance of the firelight. The sangoma came to stand in front of me, his small leather bag of witchery hanging at his side. Everyone stood up. "Inyanga" (which means The Man of The Trees) was welcomed with hand movements reaching for the sky as if they could pull it down. I felt armless. Legless. I had sat cross-legged so long there was no blood circulating, but managed a hardy American smile. When I stood up, they all sat down. It was an awkward introduction, leading with my lack of witchdoctor protocol.

These warriors were ready to share their world without temples, priests or altars. The ceremony began, inviting only the spirits of the forefathers.

Grandmother would have called this an African version of a gypsy-like reading of tea leaves. As her grandchildren, we could hardly wait to see what she saw in the image left in the bottom of the teacup. Could this have been the birth of my impulsive curiosity?

Rituals in Sand and Ceremony

The sangoma raised his leather bag of offerings to the heavens. In the other hand, he held an oxtail brush to "sniff out" the hidden physical and spiritual ailments of his somber patient afraid of black mambas. More wood was put on the fire. The smoke attracts the spirits and brings good fortune.

A necklace of seeds was passed through the smoke and placed around my neck. A tingling confidence spread over my body. A woman from beyond the circle shrieked a high pitch scream. I chose to believe it was a jubilant sound. Menzie scooted closer.

I am always trying to explain myself to myself: I am a straight-line-no-woo-woo-woman, sometimes intrigued by the idea of past lives, the clairvoyant, or an Asian fortuneteller sitting by her night lantern. Tonight, the time had come to surrender to ancestral beliefs created in sand and ceremony. Perhaps my grandfather had come to join us.

Rugged in his warrior gear and surrounded by his ancient beliefs, the sangoma projected a sudden force which enveloped me. I held my breath. Things held their breath.

The sangoma's leather bag of medicines fell in front of me. "Spoliyane khotsa," he shouted. Inside were sun-parched bones, dried guts of snake, and bark of certain trees that he would gather on moonlit nights. "These are used to communicate with the spiritual forces that actually do the work," he later explained.

Out of the bag, the sangoma pulled a small bottle and loosened the cork. Everyone clapped their hands in unison addressing the spirits with a murmured incantation. Menzie motioned for me to do the same. They folded their arms across their chests and raised their hands to the dark sky filled with smoke.

With the tiny bottle in his hand, he reached for my hand palm up. No living soul would believe this scene; but it was not the living soul I should be concerned about. As the black powder was poured in my hand, I could smell ammonia. I primed myself. I knew the next thing I had to do. My eyes squeezed tightly shut. I screwed my face up with a not-so-brave grimace and threw the powder on my tongue. I felt the powder's black dryness cling to the inside of my mouth. I could not speak and scarcely saw through teary eyes. Little blisters surfaced inside my lips. Blood pounded violently against my temples. Would hallucinations come next?

On the verge of crying I mumbled, *you got yourself into this girl, now you had better get yourself out.* I spit out the horrid pine resin aftertaste.

My face felt flushed, yet I was beginning to shiver. "Fetch a blanket." He commanded a woman from beyond the circle. She placed it around my shoulders and smiled knowingly. In the morning, I would tell myself something different, but at least now, I wanted to believe an ancestor had visited me. That is, if I woke up at all.

Sleep and sun brought new perspective.

In the months remaining I never saw a mamba, never lost my fear of seeing a mamba, and never understood the power that dwells in the African bush. However, the following new research adds to the paradox of one of the world's deadliest snakes.

From "National Geographic"

February 2013

"Researchers at the Mayo Clinic report the molecular gifts of toxic animals offer hope in the fight against a host of debilitating diseases. Heart patients owe gratitude to the green mamba, a deadly African tree snake whose venom impairs its victim's nerves and blood circulation. A key peptide from the venom was fused with a peptide from cells in the lining of human blood vessels to make cenderitide, the subject of clinical trials. It is intended to lower blood pressure in a failing heart, and shields the kidneys from an overload of salt and water. 'That is the beauty of this drug,' says Mayo cardiovascular researcher John Burnett. 'It is designed to cover both things.'

"The closely related black mamba, a snake whose open mouth resembles a coffin and whose venom can quickly put you in one, holds a toxin with huge potential to be a powerful new painkiller. Peptides from mambas will someday be used for treating heart failure."

~Jennifer S. Holland

Disappointment

Disappointment

An article written by Jeannine Antoniou for
The Times of Swaziland

September 1991

**"A wise man leaves room for likelihood
of failure in his heart."**
Ndumiso Mdziniso, Athlete

A newcomer to Swaziland, I was to eventually learn that disappointment is the rule. In America, it is often the exception. When I left last June, it was my challenge to be a part of another culture, without judgment.

Swaziland is my teacher, and lessons come every day. With disappointment always part of the curriculum, I struggle to accept and endure. I watch the Swazi people.

This last week, my teacher has been Ndumiso Mdziniso, the 400-meter runner who was to participate in the All African Games. He was dropped just days before the team departure to Cairo. When his hopes were dashed for the last time, and he accepted that it would be best for him not to go, I witnessed a courage I rarely see, especially in someone who is only 20 years old.

Ndumiso returned from schooling in Taiwan on a scholarship a month before the All African Games to prove his speed in the time trials. "As far as positioning is concerned," Ndumiso said, "we spoke to the South Africans and asked how someone with time of 46.84 in the 400 meter would place in South Africa and fare in the All African Games. We were told that this person would go as far as the final and make an impact. In South Africa he would rank 14th."

Only the official came to witness Ndumiso's time trial performance, but the other athletes were amazed at his speed despite running alone and on a dirt track. He did not know at the time, if anyone were to be dropped, it would be him. Two days before they were to leave Ndumiso and two others were told they would not be going because of a lack of funds.

Through rumor, Ndumiso understands that he was dropped because he had to face a punishment, a punishment which he feels he does not deserve. He said, "While I was in Taiwan, my coach wrote letters back here concerning my attitude about not being serious with my training and concentrating. I did have some problems in Taiwan as anyone would, especially in understanding the Chinese language. I was the only black in a densely populated community and had many nasty experiences. Sometimes they acted like something was wrong with my skin and my hair. It was tough for me to adapt, I did my best. Nike, who is my official sponsor in Taiwan and holds my scholarship, was not concerned about my behavior."

However, Ndumiso refused to give up trying to find ways to go. He was still battling an earlier allegation that he had forged his Form 5 Certificate. To prove this untrue, he requested the Ministry of Education to send his certificate straight to the Administration Office at the University in Taiwan. For unknown reasons they delayed sending it. His 3-month visa expired, so he returned home.

Helplessly, I watch Ndumiso standing tall and alone, under tremendous pressure with disappointment confronting him hourly. He believes, "if you just sit down nothing will come from the sky and drop into your hands. You have to work hard for everything."

Ndumiso ends his story. We both sit silently.

As an American, I watch women, like Margaret Kubheka, who have kept Africa alive. I learn from men like Ndumiso Mdziniso who still believes, who still hopes, realizing disappointment has served to make him strong and even more determined to succeed.

I feel Ndumiso can speak for all young Swazis when he says, "It takes a strong man to survive such hardships. We Swazis have been raised with disappointment, and I personally feel that whatever happens I take it as a challenge. We must give each other courage, for we are all fighting to raise the Swazi Flag."

Polish Priest Meets Mormon Infidel

"At night after my sweet baby boy is in bed, when the light is gone, and I see nothing it is the hardest.

I am waiting to know what it is like for the world to not have me in it any longer."

~ **Thembe 1992-2010**
A South African mother

Polish Priest Meets
Mormon Infidel

South Africa - January 2001

Exhausted, I slumped on the hard bed wrapped tightly in a rough wool blanket. Everything felt forced, claustrophobic, cornered by four walls. I pulled the threadbare sheets out from the frame of cold metal. The simple room at the monastery was filled with overpowering smells of must and mildew, which caught in my throat. "Even the air is oppressive," I murmured. It was dark, spiritless, compared to the many times I visited Zulu villages over the years. Outside I watched the sunset canonize against the gray clouds, a sangoma's prophecy of rain.

Early that morning I had traveled most of the day from Durban, which has the biggest Indian population outside of India. This huge modern city sprawled along the white beaches of the Indian Ocean. I was driven past rolling pineapple fields and pine tree forests. The sun followed us through The Valley of a Thousand Hills. "This journey over the mountains, is like a black mamba, fast, nasty, and goes where it wants to go," my Indian driver warned me. His eyes glued on the sharp curved road. My wandering mind thought back to home in Idaho, where the wildness has been taken out of lives.

Dehydrated and hungry, I knew it would be a few more hours on the road. The sky darkened. Occasional conversation helped the time pass. He began his polished introduction, "The church and monastery was built by Polish Trappist monks when they arrived in 1888." He ignored the sweat beading on my face and my hand clutching the armrest.

Nauseated by hairpin turns, I glanced at my watch. It was late. Without stars in the sky, it was difficult to see oncoming cars and the people walking too close to winding turns of the highway. "The church has given us schools, and the sisters have taught many children," he reassured me.

He turned off the road. Our headlights caught a glimpse of jagged rocks, and big boulders protecting the entrance to a graveled driveway marked **Private**. The iron gates were locked at the entry that led up to the austere red brick buildings. We waited for someone to come and let us in.

"You can see over on the right, Father Ignatious has been working by his own hands to make a proper soccer field for 1,000 young boys who come to play." It had rained the day before. Pools of muddy water surrounded two goal posts without nets. "It is his dream to build more soccer fields to keep boys out of mischief. Maybe you and the people of America can help?" I looked over at his brown face and hopeful smile.

A worthy vision, I thought. However, my second visit was to find a suitable place for the eight teens coming from Idaho and Arizona in only six months to learn and be a part of the Zulu culture. We wanted to become partners with a local orphanage or school. We arrived at the door and I thanked him, "Siyabona."

Praying Mantis

I did not know what to expect as an invited guest to the monastery. For many villages it was a living sentinel in the clouds high on a hill.

A sister greeted me at the double wooden doors. She slipped her beaded rosary in the pocket of her long black dress that modestly covered her slim body. I smiled. She looked away, graceful as she was shy. A sudden wind slammed the doors shut. From her ring of old keys, she locked both doors, and walked me to a room down a long hallway.

The room was a refuge.

Hung on a rusty nail too small was a painting of Mother Teresa. On the opposite wall above the bed, the Black Madonna hung off center and angled precariously toward the headboard. I reached up to balance it.

I felt protected until the thunder bolted through the window. A streak of lightening flashed against a praying mantis on bended knees clinging to the wall inches above my pillow.

The bare light bulb swung from a long cord. It swayed, casting a shadow on an old Bible with a ring of dust around its worn leather edges and placed perfectly on a handmade table beside the bed.

A cold breeze drifted through the cracks of the closed window. The glow from the candle flickered and dimmed into darkness. The room was black, like the Madonna, the mantis.

The Mission of Czestochowa was a place of sacred paradox, secrets kept in Old World ritual. Whispered prayers were a strange comfort for me who was born Mormon. Catholic absoluteness versus the Mormon philosophy of being the only true church had always been deadlocked. If Mother Teresa could not be accepted into the celestial heavens of Mormonism, what kind of afterlife could I expect?

The two priests from Poland (Czestochowa) lived in the monastery most of their adult years. Patriarchs among the Zulu people, they learned an African culture and language.

In my quiet room, high ceilings echoed the thick East European accent of the Jesuit priests. I imagined a candled sanctuary, penitent nuns kneeling with heads bowed, and chanting pleadings of forgiveness at the foot of the forgiver.

After a long silence gentled footsteps faded, except for someone coming my way, the heavy door opened. This was not my first time to meet the Jesuit. We were introduced by a doctor from the Valley of a Thousand Hills. I was confused by his stern welcome. He walked across the room and placed my heavy suitcase down on the pine floor. The white robe flowed close behind him. Dark hair curled slightly above his ears and eyes too blue for me to look into. Father Ignatius turned around slowly. His arms folded "in the letter of the law" were locked beneath the wood-carved cross hanging from his neck. He spoke. "You are on hallowed grounds, and a guest in this, the House of the Lord."

I would be there for two weeks.

A bold Father Ignatius kept me silent. Afraid of thoughts, a Mormon heart pounded in the religious infidel. Did he experience through some veiled Catholic clairsentience that I was an unbeliever? Should I bow and kiss the ring?

He was taller. I was older. He respected my search to find an orphanage.

I needed Africa more than it needed me

When I first came to South Africa in 1986, during the violent struggle of Apartheid, my friends wanted to believe it was a naïve passion, an obsession that would pass with time. What they did not know was I was no longer willing to sit on the sidelines as I had done the last 30 years in America's hidden Apartheid.

I had longed to be in the middle of the human condition. Many visits and extended home stays later, I began to see a better way to understand our world. Face to face, connecting our two cultures, Small Village Foundation brought high school students from Idaho to learn and work beside the Zulu students and teachers living in rural areas.

Out of my comfort zone, I learned the most. I wanted the students to see the real Africa I had come to love. I knew the surrounding villages near the mission at Centocow and the students would find ways to connect and to learn from each other.

In 2002, our Small Village Foundation* was in place, all that remained undone was to find the site of an orphanage. Father Ignatius explained to me that the people in rural areas did not believe in orphanages. He suggested a day shelter might be best.

The journey would begin in the morning. Restless, I could not sleep. From the unlighted room, I felt the chill of the fierce wind that drifted under the door. I could not see my hand or the movement of the mantis on the wall. In the silence of nothing, I felt I had abandoned myself. The phone lines were down, and I was dead to the outside world.

In the midst of a sleepless night, I saw glimpses of an ended marriage, a family lost to betrayal, and a tormented turn away from the religious beliefs of my ancestors.

I had grown up with the stories of grandmothers whose faith had pushed handcarts and carried their babies into the desolate desert of a promised land. I imagined the lineage of these women raised from behind their pioneer headstones etched by heartache and broken dreams, beside the Wasatch Mountains.

Years later, I saw such bravery reflected in my grown daughter as I stood by her as the lifeless body of her young husband was lowered into a cold Wyoming grave.

I began to drift off to sleep, second guessing decisions that time could not reverse. I fought to stay awake long enough to remember why I chose the path of Africa. A path that would lead to the side of a fevered child with malaria, or walk in the shadows of brave women like Ela Gandhi, Nonsikilelo Biko, the daughters of Alan Peyton and Nelson Mandela.**

Rain pounded the broken window, shattering memories from another time. Shivering, I pulled the thin blanket up to my chin wanting more sleep. Down the long corridor outside my room, I heard the melody of hushed rhythms. The priests were chanting in prayer the language of their Polish mothers.

I imagined how the Polish monastery called Czestochowa had been established in 1888 by the Trappist Monks. Many years later, non-black priests adorned in white declared the existence of another god. The rural people of Kwa Zulu Natal, devout in ancestor worship, were persuaded. It was said by chiefs, "This God brought from across the oceans would hear the mournful mother's tormented prayer for her children slowly starving."

Soon they would experience living in the nightmare of AIDS. An entire generation was lost. The death of the young, the death no one talks about.

* See conversations at the end of the book
** Visit www.smallvillagefoundation.org

No Stranger to Death

The morning came early. Father Ignatius had invited me to walk with him to a nearby village. He had been summoned to the village of Tobias Induna.

Leaving the quiet monastery, we walked past the borderless soccer fields. The priest came alive as he told me how soccer began in this rural area.

Father Ignatius slowed his wide stride as we climbed the steep hill that felt like a mountain with my five-foot frame lagging behind. He talked about the valley below us, and I became mesmerized by the legend of Zulu-dressed warriors lead by King Shaka. Father Ignatius stopped and sat for a while, waiting for me to catch my breath.

He pointed far off to the Valley of a Thousand Hills and the rounded thatched huts that brightly painted the countryside. Smoke rose above large black cooking pots smoldering on the wood fires.

Father Ignatius spoke quietly and his eyes betrayed sadness as he asked, "Who will care for these forgotten children, who will care for the orphans raising orphans?" The words stung. Hurled back to vivid memories, I was reminded of the purpose to find the safe shelter of an orphanage. Idaho was oceans away. Tears burned down my cheeks falling onto parched lips. The taste of salt was bitter to the thoughts of motherless children caught alone in the generations to come.

The scenes of the dead and dying were not about my sadness nor me. I remembered powerful words in an interview years ago with Nonsekilelo Biko, the widow of apartheid's slain leader: "Africa does not need your tears."

My attention drifted back to Father Ignatius and his story of Tobias.

"Tobias was my first soccer player and loved the spirit of sport. He was fast as the wind, sprinting ahead of the other players. Down the field he would run where his agile feet caught the ball. At 15, Tobias was a leader on and off the field."

Father Ignatius coached a game that he himself loved.

I did not know priests could participate in sports. Unaware in the practice of being a priest, I dared to ask, "How did you come to play competitive soccer?" Hoping this was not an out-of-bounds question, I waited in uncomfortable silence. "As a young man, growing up in Poland, soccer was my life." Soft spoken and shy, he revealed, "I became a champion, the pride of my fellow countrymen." Working with him over the next four years, I wondered why he became a priest.

We walked down the hill. I was inspired as he talked about creating a proper soccer field out of nothing but bare land.

"This would be a safe place for boys. To keep idle minds busy, I pushed them constantly beyond pain, building resilience, and to feel the fire of competition," he confided.

For the boy warriors, the vision of Father Ignatius was to reduce inborn tribal fighting that was spread like a plague in the villages. "One of the first 24 boys to join a competing team was Tobias." Our pace quickened as he explained enthusiastically that over 1,000 young lives have been transformed.

At that moment, it eased the pain I saw. He turned to face me. "Today, I have come to Tobias to say goodbye."

Zulu Mother

The air was washed clean by the night's rain. Each footstep was heavier, as we walked through deep mud. Unwilling muscles bent at my knees, the pain was difficult to hide as we came to the entrance of the village. It was unusually quiet.

Father Ignatius was no stranger to death.

The branches of the giant Acacia tree covered a mother grieving for her son. Several days earlier, she had come to visit the Polish priest who was a second father to Tobias. The concern was not for herself, but for her youngest borne and to ask for one last blessing.

The long Cossack robe hid his tired body. Age reflected lines burrowed into his face from the southern sun and another young life cut short.

We entered the straw-covered hut with its white-washed, plastered walls. Smoke filled the air and my lungs. The women of the family had been kneeling through the night at the side of the son, singing the prayers of Czestochowa and for a miracle by the priest.

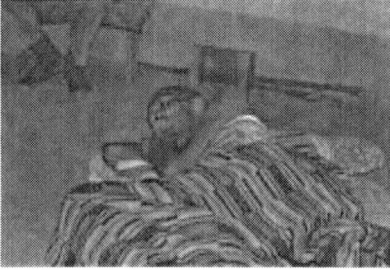

Tobias lay on a mat, covered with a checkered red blanket. His squared dark cheekbones looked chiseled out of ebony, his body slipping into a world we cannot see. Tobias was at the unforgiving mercy of the sickness no one talks about.

A freshly broken branch from the gum tree was placed at his feet, inviting the spirit of the ancestors to the side of the young man. In Zulu tradition, Father Ignatius knelt over the body of his first soccer player, speaking his adopted language, only those in the village understood.

From his thin mat, Tobias looked into the eyes of empathy; a slight smile crossed his dark lips. Father Ignatius returned the quiet gesture. I wondered if the coach and soccer player were thinking back to the days on the green field with unmarked borders.

No longer the coach, the priest led the spirit of Tobias toward another world beyond the hut. The mood was somber as the last embers of the fire were dying.

A small bottle of oil cradled in a white cloth was held to anoint Tobias. With the Holy Sacrament, Father Ignatius gently touched his forehead, pleading to the fathers who had gone before him. I listened to the sacred words in the tradition of the Zulu culture.

As I left the hut, I hoped death would be swift. Few words were shared walking back to the red-bricked mission sitting high on a hill.

Orchids and Prayers

This tall, lightly bearded man stood quietly leaning against the door of the glass framed garden shed he had built to protect the baby orchids. Father Ignatius must have felt continents away from his Polish beginnings. I wondered what turn of events brought this priest to Africa, with prayers and orchids his only companions.

As a sword is double-edged, so were my feelings left in the day's few sunless hours. I was perplexed by an increasing love for this land and on the flip side, the profound pain of too much tenderness. Could I ever come to understand nature's backdrop of tragedy and triumph, the face of cruelty and the lure of beauty in the wildness of Africa?

Many years had passed since he was walking with a friend, running out of reach from the white waves along the shores of the Indian Ocean. He had lived half a lifetime in the birthplace of mankind. The next day he would return to his Dutch home along the wide country canals near Amsterdam. I have never forgotten his last words. "In the passing years, you may wish you had never come, for the soul of Africa will break your heart, but remember, hope lays wait to teach a deeper love."

Africa moulds the unbrave in the Refiner's fire. It beckons us around the corner of the next village where orphans raising orphans call to me:

"Sawubona, Mkkulu" – Good morning grand grandmother, a term of affection.

"Kunjani" – How are you? they sing out.

"Ngiyaphila, abantwana" – I am fine, sweet children of Africa, I am fine.

The Day I was
No Lady

The Day I was No Lady

He was handsome, dangerous and unimpressed with American women. Dirk was not tall, but his skin was browned by the southern sun and his flirtatious green eyes were hidden behind aviator goggles.

Angela, his sister, was a long time friend of mine who arranged for us to meet at the Wanderboom Airfield outside of Pretoria. She said it would be a delightful experience to fly in a very rare vintage airplane for an afternoon of "swooping and soaring."

His khaki safari shorts showed his bulging leg muscles and a shirt which could have been adorned with a multitude of pilot's medals from the war in Angola. After the awkward meeting, Dirk's smile seemed to taunt the skirt I decided appropriate to wear. "Hey honey, you are gonna have to climb up onto the 43's wing," patting me on the hip.

Didn't he know this is the '90s? That unrestrained behavior was the first of many unwanted gestures that afternoon. I wished I'd said, "Put those philandering hands back in your safari pants, *Dirk, honey,* you may think I am a ditzy blonde, but I am no pushover!"

The old war bird's wing came down to my shoulders. I would have to hoist myself up no matter what now. After negotiating my way up on the wide wing, I stood for the longest time, looking high above my head and wondering if a man had named it cockpit. Perhaps a bit too independent, I had to ask Dirk for help. He boosted my legs and dumped me over the edge onto the hard leather seat. I sat in the front and could see nothing over the fuselage. Dirk's ego grew bigger as the propeller blade began to twirl.

I could tell this was going to be a power-thing between us. I had been single for 15 years and I knew my way around bad boys.

The cover over the cockpit was slammed tight. I put the headphones on and was ready. He spoke into his microphone, "The Harvard is notoriously difficult to fly well. In South Africa this plane is regarded as a 1943 National Treasure. I own one of 10 here at this airfield."

The sound of the old engine was deafening and a puff of black smoke poured out of the plane. Our climb up was steep. I could feel my skin peel back from the G-force of the near vertical ascent. Reaching a stall, he flipped over backwards into a plunging dive. Feeling my anger build at his blatant antics, I was furious about being held captive in his World War II boy-toy. "For the love of God," I screamed and then my word choice went downhill from there; words I can't remember even thinking came pouring out of my mouth into the microphone, thinking only Dirk could hear me. I heard a crackle in my ear. The control tower responded, "Everything OK up there?"

"Bring me down immediately," I demanded. With one last chauvinist swagger, he flew upside down too close to the ground. The game was over, he won. Little did I care about being a lady.

Naked at the Wedding

Naked at the Wedding

I cannot remember what I packed for the day's journey to the wedding. Whatever it was, it didn't help. Since I had arrived in Swaziland I had wanted to attend a three-day traditional wedding. The opportunity came when a trusted Swazi friend had arranged and offered to drive me up north near the border of Mozambique. After he introduced me to the parents of the bride and they had a warm drink of beer, the time had come for him to begin his long return home to Manzini. "I will be back to pick you up," were his last words.

He waved an enthusiastic goodbye and drove back down the dry riverbed that brought us to the village. I watched the dust swirl behind the old Toyota. I am sure he bounced in the hard seat all the way home.

I smiled to myself when I realized I never thought about the details of exactly how I would manage this stay in a rural village. The family walked me to where I would sleep. It would be my first time to have my own picturesque hut. A long grass thatched roof rolled perfectly down to a door-like opening. A soft light from the afternoon sun cast a shadow inside the hand-rounded walls. A raised wooden frame with long legs and a foam mattress on top had been carefully placed in the middle of the floor.

The evening bustle came to an abrupt close at 7:30 and everyone was off to bed. There was no electricity, no candles; even paraffin wax was in limited supply. I remembered my daily mantra, "I can do anything difficult for a while." By this time, the word "adventure" had lost some of its luster, and in a matter of weeks I was going back to America.

Smoke from a dying fire not far from my hut was drifting inside. Hopefully nothing else was drifting inside. What was it that King Sobuza had said? "To kill a snake would bring bad luck." I kept my clothes on and used my pajamas as a pillow. Whether my eyes were open or shut, it made no difference in the dark.

I went to sleep wondering what the next day would bring. If someone had given me a thousand clues, I could have never imagined.

Through the tiny slits of the walled hut, I could see the light of day rising over the hills from the Komati Valley. I heard women's voices coming closer. They were singing and laughing, it was time for a wedding. Within moments, three young women burst through the opening. They carried a large aluminum bowl with water sloshing from side to side. They are bringing me my bath water, I thought, "What a lovely touch of luxury in *the bush!*"

One of the women motioned for me to stand closer, another village maiden, pantomimed taking off my clothes. Over my head I pulled off my shirt. The youngest of the women with precocious confidence pulled out a sponge and scrubbed me from head to foot.

Now squeaky clean they began to dress me in full traditional regalia. First, the twenty pound pleated full skirt made of cowhide was scrunched down over my head. Then came one bright red two-inch swatch of fabric and draped it over one bare shoulder and diagonally down my upper body attaching it to my waist. A tall black beehive wig was set on top of my blonde hair and tucked under in the back. Then, strands of prickly rattles were wrapped around my ankles.

All three women stood back admiring their Swazi make over. I didn't think they had finished, because I had nothing over my chest except a narrow swatch of fabric. Outside the drumming had begun and in the distance I could hear people gathering for the festivities.

I was relieved when another woman came to my rescue. She stood in front of me and said, "Two more additions and she will be complete." Around my neck she placed a gold necklace then she slapped a hunting knife in my hand.

Out of the hut we all went. They paraded me around the village until we met up with the bride. How beautiful she looked. How naked I felt. I kept telling myself this must still be a wedding custom, and ignored the child giggling behind his mother's skirt looking at me with the biggest brown eyes.

This was going to be a very long three days.

People from surrounding villages came all through the day and into the next day bearing gifts to the seated groom. The bride stood in front sprinkling spirits of her father's best whiskey on the path of guests. Dancing into the night, they sang songs to the ancestors, inviting them into their prayer circle to bless the bride and groom.

The wedding came, and the wedding went.

Embarrassment because I did not have something to cover myself seemed silly now. It was a freeing feeling. I probably would have brought more attention to myself had I dressed in western attire. On the fourth day, I prepared to go back to Manzini. I slipped the grass sleeping mat off the foam and stepped outside to shake it. Out of the corner of my eye I saw something fly off into the air, it was a fuzzy legged creature desperately trying to cling to the end of my mat. This hairy spider was as big as my fist and scampered off into the bush. A young man laughed and said, "Hakuna Matata," not to worry. "He is only a Gray Baboon spider guarding you. He may be one of your ancestors."

By 8 AM the day was hot and the children were playing an African version of Hide and Seek. I noticed they never fought and had little to fight over. I helped the women sweep the footprints of dirt neatly around their huts. A few women went down to a river to wash clothes and hang them on the tall brush to dry. Now it was 9 AM and there was sewing to do, so I sat with them with my legs out straight while they made hand-sewn items. I didn't sew, and did not know what their conversation was about but listened, pretending I did. It was the polite thing to do and good to rest my dancing feet.

My watch said 10 AM. Only an hour had passed. I was sure my friend would soon be there to pick me up so I walked down to the dry riverbed to meet him. I looked in the distance for a cloud of Toyota dust.

Standing there on the land that is rich and fertile I smelled the burned red earth. I felt small. Only one person knew where I was. I could be in danger, perhaps I would never need to know. But it is here I have few limits.

In Swaziland now for almost a year, I promised myself to stay for a year or until my money ran out, whichever came first. I had enough money to buy my plane ticket home, and enough toilet paper to last to the end of this day.

This was a comfortable point with a few days before my final departure, everything was clear for a moment like an unintentional Zen pilgrimage. The wedding was my last Swazi wish. I began my long hike back up to the village.

I sensed a slight shift in the blue cloudless sky. Without warning, I heard the wind come down through the valley. I saw nothing.

As I reached the edge of the huts, I looked behind; the sky was a heavy brown and blowing red dust. As the cloud descended in a matter of moments, it became impossible to breathe, or see where I was going. Several women hurried me into a sheltered area and explained that these winds came almost daily. It was at least six hours before the blowing and howling died down. Later I learned they were called the Harmattan Winds.

A cup of hot bush tea calmed me for the evening. The winds probably had kept my friend from coming. I fell asleep wondering if I was alone tonight in the hut. Outside the night throbbed with crickets beneath the silent moon.

Each day folded into the same routine, sweeping dust, washing clothes, sipping tea, listening to the laughter of the chatting women, who appeared to be truly content with the pace in their lives. I wanted to hide the dull pain, the pain of nothingness. One morning melted into another morning. Days passed with nothing to distract me. Even the hands on my watch meant nothing. I felt useless. I wanted to scream "Is this African disappointment going to follow me wherever I go?" but I knew this would be useless.

After two weeks, I stopped counting how long I had been their guest. Never before had I abandoned myself from thinking, talking, or doing.

One particular morning I made my way down to the river with a handful of laundry. Close by, there was a woman on the riverbank washing clothes with a baby cuddled on her back. Her friendly smile invited me next to her.

On my knees, I leaned over the edge of the river and saw my true self, a white reflection in the water. Wordless, I asked the dangerous question, "What do I want from life?"

In my mind appeared the Leopardess who cries in the night unafraid of the dark. I remembered the African myth that surrounds her:

... reclaim that which was lost, delve into places within ourselves that need healing and face our fears in quiet stillness.

The last decade of living in the flurry of busyness, I had concealed fears of failing again. Love and longing were swept to the past. I knew it wasn't worth the risk so I put aside my dreams, possibilities and promises.

For those three weeks, I had wandered to the other side of alone. When I didn't care anymore about leaving the village, I began wondering if this had actually been a time of stilled sacredness masked in uselessness.

On the safe grounds of the village, I let myself acknowledge what I really wanted, to love and be loved. Like the Leopardess, I was ready to follow my instincts.

My tears were dry. I would cry again but not again in pained surprise.

Last Great Hero

Last Great Hero

I wondered what he was thinking holding the smooth handle of the wooden rake mindfully sweeping each dry leaf onto a meticulous pile. Was he remembering the dream he cherished when he entered prison at the age of 44, "one-person one-vote on a common voters" role? Was he regretting years lost while on his "long walk to freedom" when he spoke out against apartheid in the slaughter of his people?

Or was he thinking of those courageous men who served with him in prison, and "proud of the rebelliousness and stubborn sense of fairness he inherited from his father," which brought him a lifelong friend in Walter Sisulu.

Mandela's home in Qunu

Perhaps he was feeling saddened when he was forbidden to be with his mother when she died, longing for what might have been had he chosen to live life differently after leaving his childhood home in Qunu.

Was he thinking about how he had yearned to be home to resume a normal ordinary life, "to pick up some of the old threads of his life as a young man?" Was it the desire for his people to be free that changed "a frightened young man into a bold one?" After being in prison for so many years did he more clearly understand that the oppressor must be freed just as surely as the oppressed?

He said he never regretted his commitment to the struggle, and "was prepared to face the hardships that affected him personally." But when alone, did he ask if the price paid by his family was perhaps too dear a price for his commitment. Could a family ripped apart ever be restored? Could he say what was hidden in his heart to Winnie his wife, bold and brave for 27 years?

How can he begin a meaningful conversation with his daughter, Zanani, only four years old when he began serving a life's sentence and never allowed to visit her father, a political prisoner on Robben Island?

The same month of my birth in 1943, he first marched in support of a successful bus boycott. I was entering my freshman year at Brigham Young University, when continents away in Africa the CIA (America's Central Intelligence Agency) had just tipped off this freedom fighter's exact location to the white South African Police Defense Force who captured and arrested him. Years later he said, "I cannot lay my capture at the (CIA's) door. It was a wonder, in fact, that I wasn't captured sooner," attributing his arrest to his own mistakes.

Headlines in 1989 announced that the Berlin Wall had been torn down and months later in 1990 the South African resistance leader Nelson Mandela was released from prison after 27 years.

And now I watched this great man, a short distance away in his yard basking in a simple task alone, who often responded to crowds of people gathered around him, "… I am an ordinary man who became a leader because of extraordinary circumstances."

Slowly driving, my friend Shoki and I crossed over Moema Street onto Vilakazi Street and parked not far from Mandela's small red brick home at 8115. Shoki Motlatle was a young black South African woman who had just returned to her country after graduating from the University of Oregon in Eugene. I was staying with her family. Mandela often said, "I wanted not only to live among my people but like them." We were in Soweto, a place where everyone knows everyone, but whites never enter, South African, English or American.

Nelson Mandela looked taller, stronger and much younger than I had imagined. His broad shoulders sported a Madiba shirt, an African batik popularly labeled after his Xhosa clan name, "father of the nation."

Thick white hair framed his face, wisdom etched into deep wrinkles. A golden translucent aura was about his body. Age had only made him more handsome. I could not believe I had no camera with me and within moments I was about to meet my hero. With his "mischievous sense of humor," our smiles greeted each other as I stepped out of the car driven by a friend.

Shoki stepped forward, *Wamukelekile khaya Madiba*, (Welcome home, father of our nation) *unjani lgama ngu Shoki Motlatle magikwethule American kumama wami* (let me introduce you to my American mother). His hand met mine as it disappeared in the warmth of tenderness. His eyes, journey tired, still sparkled with a father's twinkle. That day I was the recipient of a heart without limits to the love it can give.

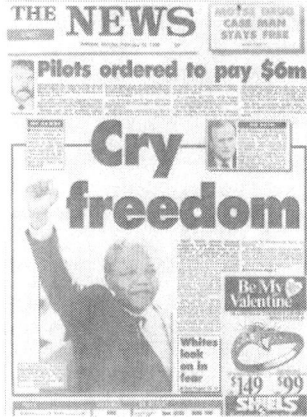

What one moment brings another moment can take away. Startled, we all heard the sudden sound of screeching brakes. He looked up just as I turned around to see a menacing patrol car pull up behind us. Growing up in the apartheid-ruled government, Shoki knew what to expect and quickly pulled me away. Two young white uniformed men of Dutch descent began shouting in the abrupt language of Afrikaans, "You women must leave immediately."

In a rush of fear and confusion I had only seconds to look back at my last great hero, a man no walls could contain. Yet, he could do nothing but humbly obey the law. The law voted on by the English and Dutch minority; the law no person Black, Indian or Colored had the right to vote in the land of their birth.

In his long walk home, Nelson Mandela has said, "The policy of apartheid created a deep wound in my country and my people. All of us will spend many years, if not generations, recovering from that profound hurt. But the decades of oppression and brutality had another, unintended effect; it produced the Oliver Tambos, the Walter Sisulus, the Chief Luthulis of our time. Men of such extraordinary courage and wisdom may never be known again. Perhaps it requires such depth of oppression to create such heights of character."

In a life of struggle, he said, "I have walked that long road to freedom. I have tried not to falter; I have made missteps along the way. But I have discovered the secret that after climbing a great hill, one only finds that there are many more to climb."

As I write these words, Nelson Mandela is only a few short days from turning 95 and continues to fight for his life. Yet, the world holds on to him. Is it part of the Xhosa custom when someone is dying the family must allow the person to ascend to the next life?

This day, July 4, 2013, I ask why is it so hard to let him go? Is he climbing his last hill or is he finally at the top looking beyond?

LONG WALK
TO FREEDOM

Mandela

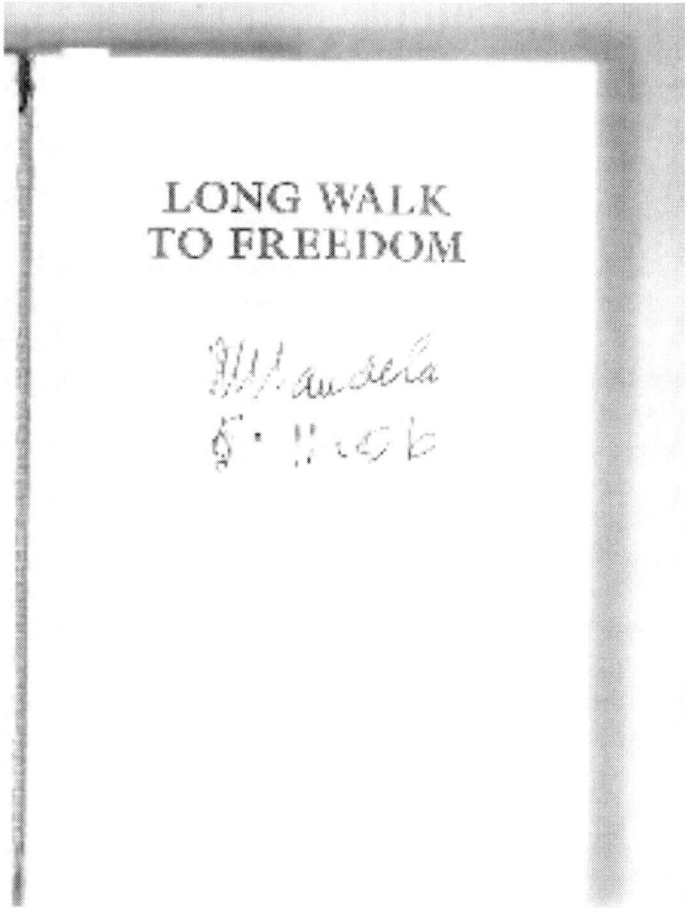

*"As I walked out the door toward
my freedom, I knew that if I did
not leave all the anger, hatred
and bitterness behind that I
would still be in prison."*

~Nelson Mandela

"*Success breeds confidence, but who has the right to confidence except for the Gods. I had a following wind, my last tank of petrol was more than three-quarters full, and the world was as bright to me as if it were a new world, never touched. If I had been wiser, I might have known that such moments are, like innocence, short-lived.*"

~Beryl Markham

Diamonds in the Palm of her Hand

Diamonds in the Palm
of her Hand

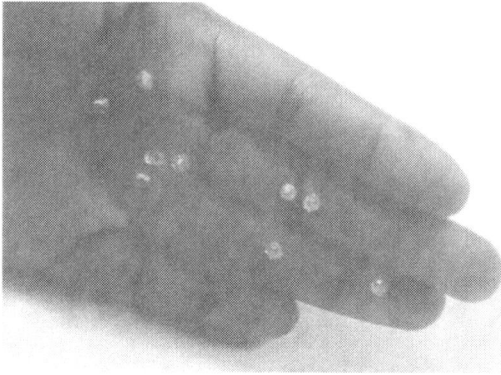

The blade of the rusty knife twirled in his quick hands. Nine tiny holes were dug into the bar of soap. Zamora must have done this many times, I thought. He knew exactly what to do.

"Finished," he said with a confident smile, and nodded for me to open my tightly clenched hand. For the last time I looked at the nine "rough" stones. Reluctantly, I handed them to Zamora.

With a little spit and few strokes of his thumb, they were embedded one by one into the openings of the soap, and $32,000 disappeared.

Zamora had studied geology at a university in South Africa. He told me diamonds are profoundly ancient. They have existed in the universe since before the formation of the Earth or the sun. Carbon, the stuff of diamonds, is the fourth most abundant element in the solar system and probably in the universe. It exists in huge reservoirs in the interior of the stars. In the violent processes of stellar evolution, the carbon suffers unimaginable pressures. I sat spell bound, listening to his every word.

"A billion years ago a barrage of meteorites pounded the infant Earth. "Can you believe," he continued, "the bombardment could have lasted some 400 million years?" I had never heard such stories. I have had these stories in my possession for a month.

"So, some of the infinitesimal diamonds that smacked into Earth aboard the meteorites could have survived. Given the way crystals grow by adding successive layers, it may be some of the rain of ancient diamonds falling to earth seeded diamonds we mine today."

The seductive power of these 10,000-year-old chunks of carbon had strangely obsessed my life. From the time I first saw them in Zamora's huge black palm, I was lost in a kind of magic I had never experienced. He held them up close to my unbelieving eyes. "You know, the diamond on someone's finger might contain as its center a dot of a jewel whose antiquity goes back 10 billion years."

His professor said that when a rough diamond is viewed through a loupe it presents an amazing miniature world, lucid in every particular. It is like examining a landscape made of crystal.

Three Months Before ...

As the morning stars lingered in the twilight of the sky, I found my way to the compound of huts. Zamora's wife would have a steaming pot of mealy meal sitting on the wooden table crafted from vegetable crates. A freshly pressed cloth lay under the bowls of porridge waiting for us. The children would be wiping the sleep out of their eyes getting dressed in their school uniforms preparing for a long hour's walk.

It was the same intense ritual every morning for many days. From a pouch hidden in my pocket, I pulled out the small package, its delicate creases folded specifically. I placed it on the table in front of us.

I unfolded the thin white paper, continually amazed at the sparkle. Content for a moment, I sipped my cup of creamy Milo Ovaltine. Then Zamora would begin to test my knowledge of their value. He did not allow for even one mistake. I had memorized their shape.

Each night in my sleep, I visualized each crystallized raw characteristic. A shadow, an opaque whiteness, or a slight shadow affected the value of the unpolished facet in the stone. To remember, I gave each a name and knew its worth.

Thursday the 12th

"I would say this has been a crash course in smuggling," Zamora boasted and flashed me a well-earned smile. "You, an unsuspicious grandmother, carrying an American passport will cross over the South African border about noon tomorrow," he said while wrapping the bar of soap in a washcloth and placing it in my hand. "Safe journey, little Gogo."

Until that moment, nothing else had mattered. I had been well prepared for the next day. Friday the 13th was circled on the calendar.

As though battling to wake from a bad dream, I turned, watching the thin-boned children playing quietly in the corner. A scene, too often sketched in a land where there is little to eat. I felt assured the money from the exchange of stones was worth the risk. Lives were already in jeopardy when the three miners, Zamora and his brothers, executed their plan to hide the diamonds one by one as they departed from their work in the king's diamond mine.

The oil-stained lantern hanging from a wire suddenly slipped off balance. Its shadow jumped against the mud walls in the thatched hut. Intense memories burst back to the afternoon when Zamora first showed me the diamonds in his outstretched hand.

I had been living in Swaziland for six months teaching English in a rural school. Each morning I trudged down a hill near a compound of picturesque earth-made roundavels. Amidst squeals of delight and red dust a gangly group of barefoot brown-bodied children ran to walk beside me. Soon I was introduced to their father, Zamora.

"And no backing out," he looked away to wrap the soap in an ordinary worn washcloth. I wondered if this comment was intended for me, or for him.

"No more warnings to be careful," his brothers chided, trying to guide the nervous chatter into a hopeful mood.

"Smuggling for a cause," sounded good, I flipped back.

He began to tell a story of risk and possibility of death if caught.

He and his brothers had taken them from the mine owned by the king. The plan was to have an unlikely person pass through the border guards and take them into South Africa to sell.

A perfectly cut ring was never on my shopping list. Now, alone in the heart of a rural *homeland* in Southern Africa, I was coming to the end of a year and the last few months of bush adventure. The nauseating smell of kerosene from the lantern above my head singed my lungs, bringing me back to the African scene in front of me. It was an unfolding drama of desperation, children raising children, and health care only for people who pay.

I had willingly become the main character in the surreptitious trade that was to take place the next day.

My stomach churned with the 'what-if-I-am-caught' scenario. However, it was too late to turn back and break the promise of a better future for these mining families.

The three men spoke long into the night. Emotion and body gestures weaved a plot I could not understand. My ears caught a couple of SiSwati words. At the eleventh hour, did they see through my naive confidence? Zamora looked for the answer to his questions in my eyes. I blinked any outward fear away.

In the lure of adventure, I had become mesmerized by the uncut diamonds he held in his hand. Unchanged since their formation, the "stones" seared into my subconscious. I imagined myself in one of Wilbur Smith's gripping novels, an undercover character in South Africa's diamond trade. I was over the border of lust, as each one of the nine diamonds disappeared into the soap.

Was it excitement or fear that would bring me to a clandestine meeting the next day in Johannesburg?

What I had come to know was the inevitable end of lives when the men die slowly in the mines breathing the deadly glass of diamond dust. Dry drilled out of asbestos it cut into their lungs, leaving them vulnerable to TB, and the fatal effects of AIDS.

Later, I walked the moonlit path back to the place I called home for the last nine months. Again I questioned deeper, why do I keep coming back to Africa, edged *into aloneness?*

I looked around my small cluttered room. The empty backpack waited on my bed. I placed Zamora's soap carefully inside the bag; a few minutes crept by, I changed its position, and buried it deeper inside the hand towel.

My hands began to shake. I couldn't concentrate. Already overreacting, my mind bolted ahead to the next day's border crossing. I was going deep into the middle of the world's largest continent. White-on-black politics demanded desperate times at the end of South Africa's apartheid years. How close would I be inspected by the Afrikaans border patrol? These were the people originally of Dutch descent and who ruled the government. I could not stop rehearsing what could happen to me.

I couldn't shake the warning of my South Africa friend, Liz, who said "The politics of South Africa are so inflamed, if you get caught they will put you in prison to vanish your existence from the awareness of the world."

I started to second-guess the mind of the faceless person at the border, when the pack was opened.

With only a few hours of sleep left, I convinced myself to move the diamond-studded bar of soap under my leopard cotton pajamas out of sight. Exhausted, I zipped up the bag, tired of dreams, adventure, and diamond lust.

Friday the 13th

Journey with the Diamonds

All I remember was the date, Friday the 13th, the middle of the summer in 1990, and I was on a mission. For months I was coached on how not to draw attention to the lightness of my skin, the oddity of traveling by myself, and to absolutely give no outward appearance to make me look suspicious. *Do nothing that could reveal why I was going into Johannesburg.*

The three Swazi miners whose families I had befriended sternly cautioned me, "You must not even think about what you are doing. Those clever border guards can read your mind and smell your fear. And they don't like Americans."

I felt like I could do anything. At this point, I was ready to face anyone or the fear no matter what.

The morning was dark as I approached the empty Toyota kombi. "When do you leave?" I asked the dozing driver.

Startled, he glanced at his watch and said, "When the bus is full," which sounded logical, but not helpful at the moment. This did not fit into my careful Plan A. Forty minutes later we were driving south toward the border leaving the little town of Manzini, located in the heart of Swaziland in South Africa. It was a time of hope and joy for the "New South Africa" and surrounding countries to look beyond the tragic racial killing of the post-apartheid years.

My first warning began when the tired engine started lurching. Like a gunshot, the muffler backfired. Everyone tried to calm each other down. Acknowledging the mishap, they nodded to each other. A deep laughter rumbled with uneasiness. I had learned during the year of being in this Swazi "homeland" to take note of this flip-side reaction.

I felt reassured. These passengers had made room for me, a foreigner, beside them. They accepted my American ways, treating me as a woman like themselves, alone on our way to somewhere not far away.

Johannesburg, South Africa, was a 6 to 8 hour drive.

The bright sun came through the shaded side of the window; a woman sitting next to me opened the newspaper, "The Times of Swaziland." In a loud voice, she began reading everyone's horoscope for Friday the 13th. I wondered if in Swaziland, there was a supernatural meaning to this date. "What does it say for a Virgo?" She read to me:

Usually so logical, so practical, today you are way off your mark, and by pushing ahead, you may get yourself deeper and deeper into problems. The letter P is important.

This was a horoscope for the Swazi people. It was too late to worry. No matter how I interpreted the message, I was not going to let it ruin my day.

I know I will be patted down by unfriendly suspicious guards. It has been drilled into the minds of the Afrikaans people to be suspicious of Americans, we who initiated the world to place crippling economic sanctions against their country; we who were fighting for the release of Nelson Mandela.

My mind jolted back to my new friends in the Toyota. Maybe Friday the 13th was like any other day. Nothing could be suspicious about the chickens on their laps, or holding bundles of garden vegetables ready to sell at the market.

The women began singing as they always do in tense times. It calmed me. "*Siyatibonga Tonkhe Tinhlanda*," *we give thanks for all our good fortune.*

In between songs the stories began. The woman next to me was married to the attending physician of "the old king," as they called him. She said, "King Sobhuza II taught his people that no one is better than anyone else. He ruled for 78 years without war." I thought, this is the answer to peace in the world.

They argued about how many wives he had, 77 or 82. "Whatever, he loved them all," a woman in the back of the bus spouted. "One time he even left a love note before he left his fourth wife's hut."

"Sometimes the wives would be lucky to have a hand-written poem or a thank you scribbled on an egg." This journey was more full of fun than Friday the 13th superstitions.

An hour before the border patrol, our kombi broke down. I couldn't believe how quickly the scene changed. They filed out through the door resigned to this common occurrence and sat beside the road to wait for help. Where would the help come from, their prayers, or the witch doctor's bottle of muti magic they carried in their pocket? I thought impatiently.

I simply could not wait. There was no choice, I had an appointment which had been set between several men who worked at King Mswati's diamond mine with someone I didn't know, except for his name.

I put my backpack on and said my goodbyes as the hopeful women wished me well. I began walking toward the border.

It was not long before a family pulled over and offered me a ride into Johannesburg. Great luck. My horoscope didn't count as I was in Africa not America.

We arrived at the border patrol. I remembered what the miners told me: "It will be a puzzle for them, and wonder what this American woman is doing in Swaziland. Don't say more than you have to. They will open your back pack and examine everything closely, even the bar of soap that hides the nine uncut stones."

It wasn't until the next day that the surprising reception of the border guards was the only easy situation on my Friday the 13th. Unscathed and proud of a somewhat convincing performance, I met the family on the other side of the gates and continued our drive on into downtown Johannesburg. I gave them the Hillbrow address where I was to meet the mysterious contact. They were gracious, but were reluctant to drive further into a part of town that was crime-ridden and had recent warnings of an unpeaceful Zulu march. Appreciating their concern for me, they conceded to let me off at the corner well before the chaotic kombi taxi area.

I had come far but instinctively knew I had much further to go. As I closed the car door tight I heard the clicks of the locks. Behind my farewell smile, fear dropped like lead to the pit of my stomach. I steadied my walk up the concrete stairs and gripped onto the steel handrail with the frayed ends of my strength.

What I didn't know was a short distance away, many streets in the surrounding areas were swallowed up by angry mobs spilling into the center of Hillbrow. They were incited by the powerful demands of their Zulu chief Mangosuthu Buthelezi. He felt his tribe, being the largest black African tribe, had been purposely ignored by an unjust white ruling government. Wild chanting and piercing cries grew louder as I cautiously walked toward my destination. Within several blocks, I rounded the next corner and thought it wise to quickly step out of harm's way into a covered arched doorway.

This formidable scene could have been spliced out of the movie about Chaka Zulu, infamously known as the bloodthirsty African warlord whose political policy in the 1820s was murder. Unchanged by time, the fearsome dressed warriors with painted faces carried short spears and big shields of cowhide. With raised heavy wooden clubs called knobkerries they came down the street in front of where I stood in a frenzied trance of the toi-toi dance of protest.

The signage on the door, Hillbrow Shoes for Men, was a clue that I was in the right neighborhood. I went inside and asked to use the phone to call my contact. A woman's voice on the phone said her brother, Peter, had returned to the warehouse. I mentioned my transportation was delayed in Swaziland and was sorry to have missed my appointment with Peter. Nervously I quoted the warehouse address in my notebook. She asked if I would wait for her to call Peter and call back.

"Peter…" I suddenly remembered my Virgo horoscope warning, *The letter P is important.* The phone rang and the clerk handed me the receiver. "Please meet Peter at the Fontana Inn a few blocks away."

Outside the toi-toi protesting commotion had moved on. I slipped out the door and was finally on my way to meet Peter. I walked through the door of the Inn and looked around, wondering how I would recognize this man. Surely he would recognize an out-of-place, puzzled American woman standing around.

I had not waited long before I saw a man come into the reception lounge. He spotted me immediately. His gregarious smile buoyed up my lagging confidence.

As we sat and talked I felt less naïve about the big city of "Joburg" and a few steps closer to the cloaked world of the diamond trade. Peter asked how I was doing after the big protest and said the evening news had reported it was the biggest Zulu protest march in South African history. As Peter was a white guy, I was surprised when he said he hoped the government would take notice of these people whose leader was once the great Chaka. Fascinated by the passion for his country and wondered about his accent, I wanted to ask more questions but since Americans are known for asking too many questions, I just listened.

Curious, I attempted to read his body language – definitely gallant, considerate, confident, well mannered, and far too handsome dressed in white linen slacks. I ignored the hard muscles outlined under his pressed black t-shirt. Peter *seemed* kind hearted, yet it was odd that a stranger would act like he cared if I lived or died in Johannesburg. I reminded myself, "Don't get swayed by his charm, keep the walls up, head on straight, and the mystery moving."

I had not eaten all day and couldn't think clearly. My mind raced ahead of the conversation and questioned the purpose of the evening. Peter noticed my distraction and suggested we have dinner. He guided me into the dining room of the Inn, I could feel the allure of his warm body and his hand ever so slightly touching my back.

Nervous at the waves of electricity sizzling through my body, I wished Peter was not so good looking, much older, and terribly overweight. He broke through my power of concentration and began talking about being born in Portugal. His parents died in a car accident when he was twelve and he was raised by his grandmother. Later his oldest sister, who lived in the Northern Province of South Africa, insisted he come live with her. After graduating from the University of Rustenburg he was employed by the mines as a hydraulic engineer.

A hydraulic engineer dressed in linen slacks? Shouldn't he be wearing faded blue jeans worn at the knees? I wondered why he didn't ask me any questions. Who did he think I was, besides being a brave bystander during a Zulu protest, or a bored American woman smuggling diamonds? I felt a bit indignant and second-guessed. As dinner ended, I realized how late it was and excused myself to make a room reservation. I returned to the table to thank him for dinner and say good-bye.

On the way back to the table, I had two thoughts: the safekeeping of my diamond studded soap, and that as a woman on her own in Africa, I did not have the luxury of a distracting dalliance.

To my surprise, Peter was standing with his Adonis smile. I am always taken back when a man stands as I come into a room. I reached out my hand to thank him then he bent down and gave me a hint of a kiss on the cheek. As I reluctantly pulled away he handed me a paper folded in half. "Tomorrow you will need this map to the warehouse. I won't be there. Be on time, these guys are not from South Africa. They are all about business and have no patience to wait for anyone or anything."

Peter turned and walked out of the room. Such a strange sudden close to the evening, yet I knew I would never see him again.

Now in my room away from the mysterious meeting, it was important to sleep. Morning would be hustling me out of bed before the wake-up call.

With no time for breakfast, I left the Fontana Inn and walked a short distance. Following Peter's hand-drawn map, I was soon in front of the two-story warehouse. The aging dark red building, number 4901, was in a deserted industrial area. A steel-fortified door was slightly open. I climbed the steep wooden stairs, my footsteps echoing. I reached the last step and continued down the dark corridor toward the noise of a boisterous conversation spoken in a language I didn't recognize. In a matter of seconds there was silence, an uncomfortable silence. I walked through the opened door very "business like" and without hesitation introduced myself.

There were three men, as Peter had confirmed. The oldest, big, unshaven and wearing a sweat-stained shirt, did all the talking. As he came close, the heavy smell of musky rum mixed with pungent cologne saturated the air in the stuffy room. The younger guy, slumped in his chair, was angry about something. His eyes darted around the shadowy room. Above, the high windows allowed for little light, fogged over with years of grime. In a crusty demanding voice he said, "Let's see what you have."

Something bad could happen here slipped through my mind. Barely able to stand, my nearly paralyzed legs guided me over to the vacant chair. Now was the time to be the boldest I have ever been, until I caught a glimpse of the top part of a revolver tucked behind the belt on the third guy's baggy pants. In sheer panic I realized this is not going the way I had rehearsed. The young guy leaned over, grabbed my bag, and unzipped the top. Agitated, all he could see was personal clothing neatly folded. "We were told you have something for us?" he blurted.

"Of course." I desperately searched for the wrapped soap. When my fingers touched Zamora's cloth, I deferred the sheer panic to run away and forced myself to remember what the miners had risked to collect these diamonds. I had no choice but to place the treasure of stones on the table. Clam handed, the big guy snatched the soap, slid his revolver across the table between me and the angry guy and left the room.

The revolver and the demeanor of the men erased thoughts of later describing the attributes of the diamonds. Instead I wondered if I would be alive at the end of the day.

Why the gun? Was it necessary? Surely they would not use the gun, would they? Where does Peter fit in all of this? How gullible can I be? What did I get myself mixed up in? Questions ricocheted in my head; the dead-ended answers left me cold. This was like the worst nightmare. There was no waking up. My brain refused any outcome.

The two men stood up quickly when we heard footsteps. Afraid to turn around I could smell him. Grabbing the revolver he shoved it in his pants, and announced they were leaving. There was finality to this bizarre encounter.

"In an hour," he looked at his watch, "you can leave after we are gone." Stunned in disbelief I could not understand what had just happened, let alone try to explain when I arrive back in Swaziland without the money. My energy was gone, words were gone, and they were gone.

At the end of a battered silence, I struggled to lift the dead weight of my body out of the chair. I vividly remembered this feeling once before as a child, the day I strayed into quicksand. I felt my ankles being sucked down first, then up to my knees and within moments, I was being buried deeper. The more I fought the more futile it became. My grandfather heard my screams, ran to the edge and with a long branch he pulled me to safety.

This time there was no one, no screaming, no branch and no grandfather.

There I was, somewhere on the second story in an empty warehouse, still alive. The next step I told myself was to go safely down the stairs. I listened for familiar voices and moved vigilantly toward the steel door.

I had to fight guilty feelings as I walked back near the location of the Fontana Inn. I was two days late, Zamora must have known something went horribly wrong. Maybe he wondered if I had taken the money and left the country. How was I going to face them? I had failed miserably.

This was neither the time nor the place to feel sorry for myself or wonder about the preposterous idea of exchanging diamonds. It was time to find transportation back to Swaziland and to face Zamora. I was numb as I checked back through the gates of the border. There would be no questions asked by the Swazi guards only the genuine greetings of smiles and a "Welcome back" as they checked my U.S. passport.

Two hours from home, I was still piecing together a fragmented story of my messy mistakes. I pictured walking toward the homes of Zamora's family and seeing the faces of disappointment in the men. The lost hope for their children's education was now gone. My heart was heavy and my head ached.

As the signposts passed, and home came closer, it became more difficult to think of the words I would speak. Nothing I could say would ease my thoughts when we would come face-to-face with the ragged edges of my story.

Would Zamora ask himself if he chose the wrong person? Would he think the long nights of planning and preparations were a useless waste of time? We would go over and over the signs I missed along the way. He would ask endless questions about Peter and the men at the warehouse. Torn details in my memory were already beginning to fade.

Upon arriving in Manzini, it was best to see Zamora immediately. The children were playing outside when they saw me. With screams of delight, they all came running, Zamora and his wife close behind them. After the hugs, Zamora walked beside me. He looked worried, asking if I was harmed in any way.

"I am okay. But it was terrible. I don't have the money and the diamonds are gone."

"We know, what is important is that you are safe," his wife reassured me.

"What do you know?" I was very confused with her answer. "How do you know?"

"When you didn't come back the first night, we knew something had gone wrong."

"So many things went wrong. I am sorry I have nothing to show for all the work you did."

We went inside the house. The light from the lantern on the table was comforting as we huddled. More relaxed, I began to tell the story of the Toyota breaking down, hitchhiking, the border guards, the Zulu uprising, the men, and the gun. Zamora stopped me. "We were blinded by our concern for you, and decided to ask the sangoma who can see what we cannot see. When she threw the bones, the ancestors revealed your story."

I could not even begin to fathom what I just heard. "Zamora, I have great respect for the healing gifts in the mysterious world of sangomas, but beyond that I simply do not believe she had the power to actually have seen what happened in the warehouse."

"Little Gogo, there are many things in this life we cannot explain. It is like the story of the 'rough,' the diamonds you carried. There are many unknowns in each facet that is viewed, and therefore cannot be judged. I have something for you to take home, it is my last rough. It has the power to bring you back to Africa. Remember, ultimately, clarity cannot be seen by the naked eye."

In the few days I had left to be in Swaziland, Zamora's words began to rest on my mind. As I packed to leave, I hoped time would bring a peaceful closure.

The last morning I awoke early, thinking I was ready to go. I wondered if I would ever return to the people I had come to love and the land whose difficult paths taught me to leave betrayal and bitterness behind.

Outside the air was clear. The red bougainvillea trailed along the fence where Menzie was waiting to say goodbye, bravely holding back his eight-year-old tears. He came over to hold my hand for the last time. I looked around me. In the distance I remembered the encounter of the ominous mountain where the kings are buried; and just beyond the school of rowdy boys, of snakes and sangomas and places where I left pieces of myself.

Menzie and I stood near the nemesis hill I climbed each morning in broiling heat. This was the hill I hated when the pain in my legs ached more than the longing in my heart, the hill where the tears I left have long burned into the red earth.

On this lovely day, my struggle for survival seems like a small bump on a far away road. A little hand tugged on mine. "Oh, Menzie I will miss you very much. One thing for sure … I will not miss that dreadful hill."

"Auntie, we should say goodbye to the hill and walk up one more time. You will not miss the hill as much as the hill will miss you."

"There are three things extremely hard: steel, a diamond and to know one's self."

~ Benjamin Franklin

Conversations

Conversation with Pamela Mills

Granddaughter of Alan Paton, author of
Cry, the Beloved Country

August 1990

God made rivers to meander for a reason.

~ A Bushman Song

Three expired passports tucked in the back of a drawer in my bedroom, I still wonder why I push to find meaning and return to South Africa.

Why talk to Pamela Mills? How did I get this interview..I cannot remember, it was before email. I love a story.

Conversation: "Is it the rich, rich pain?, questions a granddaughter. My Sotho name is Imaneleng, which means, I listen to you. When my baby daughter was born, we gave her the Zulu name, Thandiwe, it means loved one. We wanted it to make a statement within the white community where it is so closed.

I might be white, but we are all really African, it is woven into our stock. There seems to be something passed down..in the blood..this passion. It is not tangible..a strong gut thing inside. I am committed to its differentness.

The land itself..it is a part of the earth. There is a pulsing, something about the red sun, the red earth. It is so alive and strong it haunts you. When I travel overseas, it feels tame. Pale. Here there is wildness. I'll never leave.

It is the salt with the sweet.

My father loves the Bush. He gets excited about the night sounds, like a child.

He loves the hot sun of Africa."

It was 1990. In South Africa, President F.W. de Klerk had announced Nelson Mandela would be released from prison the next day. After 27 years he had walked the Long Road To Freedom. The world waited. He emerged a hero. The world's hero.

I sat listening to Pamela, her red hair red fell about her shoulders. Together we talked into the late afternoon. Open like her father. Tender like her mother and passionate as her grandfather.

"That is a great tribute to your father, Pamela. What do you think he learned from his father?"

I edged deeper.

She hesitated, and looked away.

"I am not sure. He was at boarding school during his young life. He pleaded with his father not to send him away to the school. He became resentful, angry, and resistant to anything from his father."

The room was quiet I did not want to interrupt this pain, her pain.

"The rich rich pain." She repeated. We both breathed deep in the silence.

A professional dancer, Pamela sat poised. This graceful young mother spoke softly. Hands folded in her lap, fingers intertwined, in remembering her father.

"He was always seeking love from his prominent father, who was only sympathetic and compassionate with the characters in his books.

It is the salt with the sweet", she whispered.

I watched her eyes hold back the tears, broken hearted.

"Even though my respected grandfather was internationally known as an author, it didn't overshadow my father's life. My father did learn and valued some things from his father.

When my grandfather was headmaster of a black reformatory for young boys, he had the fence torn down. He had many black friends, always a sense of humor..it is incredible that he felt so passionate as a man. He could only express it in his writing.

I haven't read all of my grandfather's books. The reason I didn't read CRY, THE BELOVED COUNTRY, was because it tore at my heart. Each time I got to the part where the priest visits his son in jail..I couldn't read any further. It was full of all the tragedy we felt in South Africa.

Eventually I did read the book. When I was preparing for my teacher's diploma, I had to give a lesson on the book's message. I had to lock myself up in a private place. I wept and wept. It touched the deep deepest part of the pain.

It is in the same fifty-year period, when the young African boy goes to New York, in his suit made out of blanket. He felt so smart, until being laughed at by the American kids.

I find this extremely tragic. The boy is little. His dignity stripped. The meager provisions from his family, was all he has to keep up his dignity."

In the fragile moment of truth's story we sank, drowning in an uncomfortable silence. In her home in suburbs of Johannesburg, we were a safe distance from the villages of hopelessness. A place unmapped. The huge townships of Soweto and Alexandria. Our minds connected, remembering the scenes of death. Chapters painted in the blood of her country's past.

Injustice and fear would bring many more deaths in the years to come. Pamela had grown up a witness of man's inhumanity to man.

A hundred years of immigrant dogma. A cruel system of apartheid was born in South Africa. At the wooden pulpit, the Dutch Reform Church barricaded behind superiority and separateness.

It felt odd, and foreign to me. Unaware at the time, I would soon learn that this same unjust system was in my own country. The subtle slavery of today's American roots, was under the surface. I was white. Born in the land of the free, I assured myself. Unaware of my own Mormon history, I chose to close my mind."

Pamela stood up, folded her crisp white napkin and placed it on the table.

"This is my great grandmother's table that was shipped when she came to South Africa.

Would you like a cup of hot tea?"

While living in South Africa, the comfort of a cup of hot tea, with a splash of milk and a teaspoon of sugar eased a moment's transparent tension. Seeking the English composure in the pain of too much tenderness, she walked past the sunny warm window into the kitchen.

I glanced at the newspaper on the long coffee table in front of me. It was dated August 22, 1990. Near the bottom of the front page, a familiar headline caught my attention.

President Saddam Hussein said ten days earlier, he was ready to resolve the Gulf crisis if Israel withdraws from occupied territories. The second paragraph, in bold print, "President Bush calls up the military reserves."

I thought, *we all live in a changing world, founded in fear.* We were standing at attention to protect our American borders in the poor countries we conquered. Impassioned by Glory, Guts and Guns we prepared to spill the Muslim blood of young Iraqis, or to fight beside the Jewish sons of Abraham, the chosen one.

My country crossed foreign boundaries aided by a power hungry secret society, the Central Intelligence Agency. We were told, they were crushing communism in South Africa. They pledged to find and bring to justice a fighter named Nelson Mandela.

These were unprecedented times. Our own civil rights movement continued. Dr. Martin Luther King, Jr. branded a communist, and also was assassinated. We were a country whose wingspread covered the dark prison of Robben Island. The place where many Nelson Mandela's face the cold winds of winter, alone on the southern tip of the African Continent.

"Would you like English Breakfast or Roses tea?" Pamela asked.

1990 Interview with Alice and Ntsikie Biko

I decided that I wanted to meet the widow of Steven Biko, the man whose murder began to overthrow the rigid rules of apartheid. I began making phone calls in Johannesburg and was able to reach the law office that helped to try the case. Within minutes of getting her phone number from the law office, I called and spoke to Ntsikie Biko. I introduced myself and said I would be honored to meet her. She agreed immediately. I hung up the phone in disbelief and called to again to make sure I really heard what she said. A week later, I met her in King Williamstown and we talked for several hours. Just after midnight, she said that we should go over to Steven's mother's home. What follows is the conversation I had with both of these great women.

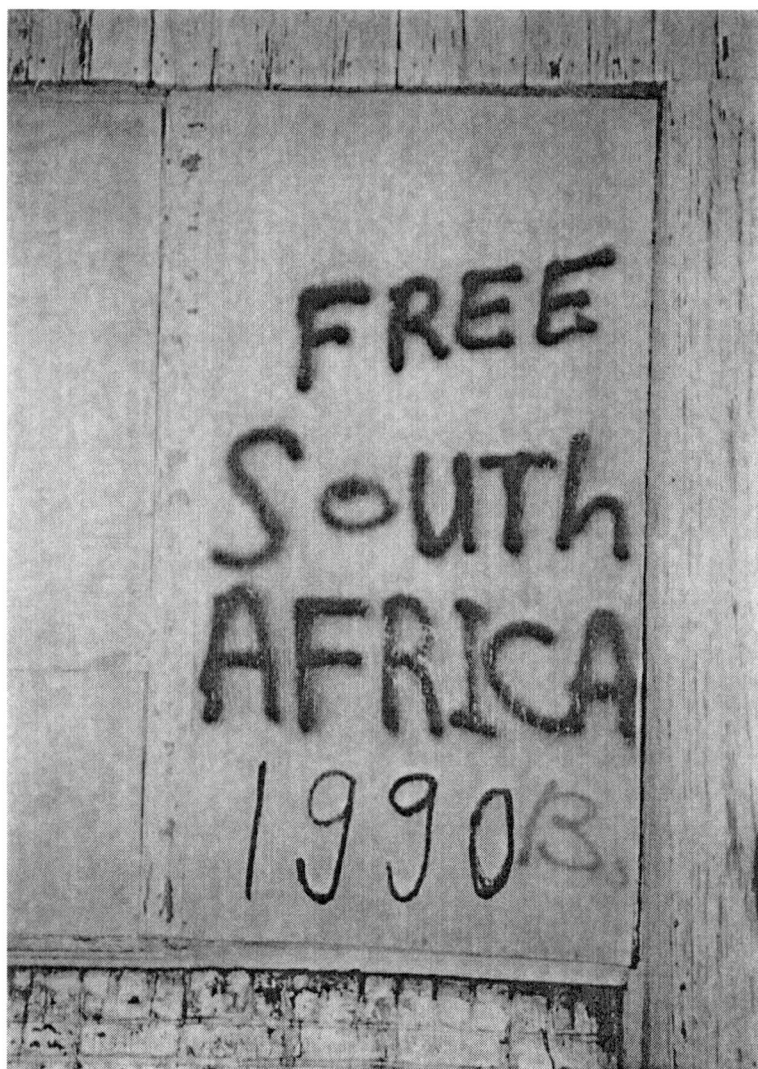

J: Jeannine

NB: Ntsikie Biko (Widow of Steven Biko)

Alice: Alice Mamceto Biko (Mother of Steven Biko)

J: Do you believe in justice?

(Both women begin laughing a deep laugh, their bodies don't disclose their thinking, and exchange long glances at each other)

NB: ...If there is any justice...is there?...There is not. (an exchange of long glances to each other).There is not justice, so you can't believe in something that is not real. But still there is hope...hope that things are going to change.

J: But Ntsikie, how can you hope when hope has been bashed over and over again with the murder of your husband?

NB: You keep on hoping. I say to myself, Steve was striving for liberation. I'm sure it will be enjoyed by our great grandchildren, not by us. When I look on years back, our fathers were shouting the freedom is not coming Africa. It's still not coming, but it's not far, it is coming.

I want to say, with the number of people that have died fighting for this, I am sure God is there, God is there to hear people's cry. We have been oppressed for years now. At least some type of happiness must be brought to us.

J: I wonder how much God can take?

NB: That is a good question. I wouldn't like to say. He is not there…Then I think, He is there…He is there!

(Steve's mother Alice Memceto Biko began to share her feelings in Xhosa, Mandela's language)

Alice: We must read the Bible. Look at the time now and look at the time of Israel. It took 40 years! Even with us today we know that God is with us. Look at what is happening all over the world. If we pray and believe in Him. God will keep us out of this condition.

J: Maybe, the struggle ends with death?

NB: You must suffer first before you can sing. Every Sunday when I look at the churches, most of the churches belong to whites, they are full from morning till evening, they are praying. They think they own Him, that they posses Him. Maybe we should too. They portray God as white. Nobody knows how God looks.

Alice: He created human beings, not blacks and whites.

(Alice laughs, a knowing laugh, a Xhosa laugh)

J: You are so beautiful when you laugh Alice. What a great mother you were for Steve.

NB: You know it is our custom – there are things you can't do and things you can do as a daughter-in-law, but with her she is like my own mother. I am just like a daughter with her. I don't feel like I was married to her son, but born as her daughter.

J: I am so happy you have each other. Alice how would you like another daughter…an American daughter?

Alice: Yes, yes. I will give you a name in the African tradition, "Noluthando".

NB: That is a good name for Jeannine, we will call her "Thando"... it means love...the love that brought you here to South Africa.

J: Thank you both. I will always remember this name. But, there was also anger that brought me here. Anger...anger against the South African system of apartheid. The policemen!

Alice: No, no Thando... it was love that brought you here... especially to us.

J: It is difficult to forget what they have done to you and so many others.

NB: If you would have come in the 1970's, you would never have seen a visitor here in Soweto, our black township. They would tap all our phones. I always felt bad for the people who would come to see us, they would be harassed.

J: Can you talk to me about the inquest into Steve's death?

NB: We felt by having an inquest we'd get at the truth. The truth was there! But because of the policemen, there were many things to hide. The government is there to protect them not the public.

The end was terrible. As we sat there the last day of that case...they were too shy to look at us. That alone made me feel that they were feeling guilty about Steven's death. We sat for days listening to their lies and excuses.

(It was 1pm, the house was cold, and Ntsikie and Alice sat in silence. For a long time, I waited in silence.)

NB: One day sometime ago, I was not at home. My mother tells me that a local security man came with a face that was very familiar to her. He kindly wanted to know if she was getting any pension money.

This face happened to be one of the policemen from Port Elizabeth. He had been with Steve and had seen everything that happened.

We were told the story, that by the time they took Steve from PE, he was still alive. They just wanted him to be away from them. Jimmy Kruger, who was minister of police then, said before the inquest 'it left him very cold.'

In Pretoria a policeman shot himself. Later when we got the story, that policeman wanted to tell the truth. He never shot himself. They shot him. He was the white policeman who came to my house that day. We will never get these stories, so many lies.

There was the day of the verdict...I think that was the worst day...I just couldn't take it. It took hardly five minutes. The magistrate came in, he stood and said, "Steven Biko died in detention on such a such date...***no one is to blame***...court dismissed."

I cannot talk anymore... I really want....

But, here we are, my mother says "God gives people strength." I pray to God that one day...one day the truth will come about Steve.

J: When I come to South Africa, I have sometimes imagined walking up to the door of the person responsible for Steven's death. I see myself at a door. It opens, In the doorway he stands, I say, "You, Colonel Harold Snyman made sure Steven Biko was killed." He looks at me with a stony stare and closes the door.

Alice: Even if, *that man* comes through my door and says, 'I am the man who did this.' That would be good enough for me. I will sit and pray for him.

NB: Ngingakkupha, can I give you some tea?

(Nsikie excused herself. There were no words to say, or think. In moments I hear the teakettle whistle. We have a cup of tea.)

NB: I must say, we're happy the way the outside world took this. They were quite supportive. Donald Woods played a very brave part. He was the editor of the Daily Dispatch, some were calling the newspaper the Daily Biko. Even Donald himself admits that he was not the right person to write about him. The only people who can write about him are the people who worked with him.

J: Do they live here?

NB: Some of them do. Steven's friends say "we are not writers, we may have an idea but to actually be able to put it down is almost impossible." What about your writing, Jeannine? You want to write about being in South Africa?

J: Writing is hard, especially when you try to connect emotion with the story. Sometimes the emotion is so strong I sit paralyzed, and nothing gets written. It takes true courage. I hope to write about this interview with you and Alice, someday.

NB: It was courageous of you to come to South Africa again. Since your first visit was so unpleasant. When you called me, there was something in your voice that made me feel there was a purpose for your visit to us.

J: When I called you initially, it was surprising you said "yes." In fact, after I hung up, I thought your response may have been only in my imagination. That's why I called back immediately to double check.

NB: Usually when I am asked for an interview, I turn them away.

J: Alice, we have had some good laughs…some cries…*Angibongi nakubonga, I can't thank you enough*. It was gracious of you to have me, a stranger in your home. When Ntsikie and I came knocking on your door after midnight I was surprised she didn't call first.

Alice: My daughter is welcome anytime, and you too, Thando. *"Inyang' ihlekwe zinyoni!"*

NB: She says, *"Tonight the moon is laughing at the birds!"*

J: I hope to return to South Africa again, I will have your voice on my tape recorder and think of you often.

(Alice laughed her deep laugh, and gave me a love-good-bye-hug.)

Alice: I will be waiting here.

(As the door closed behind us, I was sad knowing there was a good chance I would not see Alice again.)

NB: ...and she will be waiting, and remembering you. Tomorrow, I would like to take you to the cemetery where Steven is buried.

(The following interview was recorded as we walked into the cemetery with Ntsikie's son Samora.)

Samora was being so brave. He helped me through the tangled barbed wire fencing. The ground was rough, unforgiving as we walked toward the grave of his father. I felt as though I was in a dream, that it wasn't really me taking these steps beside Ntsikie, sacred cries now silent. I could sense the burden of death, as we approached the headstone.

The early morning sun was slow to rise. There was a crisp chill in the air. I could hear each footstep pressing into the cold earth.

J: I wish I had some flowers, Ntsikie…something to give…

NB: umm….mm

(There were flowers…mementoes…small rocks circled the length of the grave.)

NB: People involved in the struggle have remembered.

It was too quiet. Had I come too far? Had my white tears of this morning, entered into a black world that was not mine to enter?

J: Ntsikie, perhaps Steven doesn't have to struggle anymore?

NB: I think he is still working where he is, because most of the changes happened after he was brought here.

J: Samora can you remember your father?

Samora: I was too young.

He stood tall.

J: I can see by your face, you remember something.

NB: …his father spoiling him… when Steven took Samora to work, his secretary would say, "no, no I am no babysitter. You can't bring your son here. Now I have to wash his napkins in the office.

Samora: I was only two years old when my father died.

J: You have grown into a brave man, at 15. Your family has shown you how to be strong. I am sure your father is never far from your side.

(We walked back to the car. Many thoughts flooded my mind.)

J: Ntsikie, at times when it is really hard, I wonder how to be strong. We don't know how we will react...when our heart takes us.

NB: Our hearts know the way. Now it is your turn to be strong.

With love
From: Mrs Ntsikie Biko

A note from Nontsikelelo Biko

Jeannine's first meeting with
Ela Gandhi - 1990

Interview with Ela Gandhi.

Granddaughter of
Mahatma Gandhi

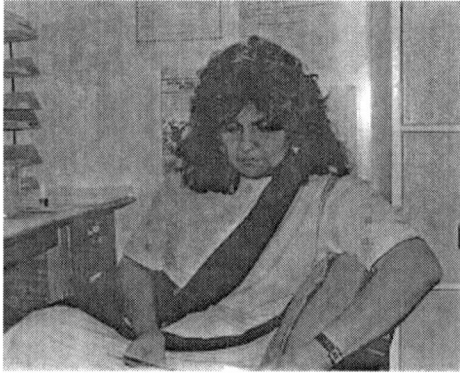

June 2011

South Africa, at Ela's home 2:30 pm

Jeannine: *As we began the interview, I summarized the theme of my book about change over the years and the lessons we have learned, looking back how we keep balanced, knowing there is a flip side to everything.. stories about my 25 years of coming into and out of South Africa; and what I've learned., 10 yrs started ago a foundation in the US that brings high school students to learn about the South African cultural diversity.*

We had a great interview several weeks ago with George Bizos, sharing the same Greek cultural background our visit was one I will always remember. He has done so much for the people of South Africa. He also speaks highly of you, Ela.

J: I am interested in how you envision your religion, and how you see traditional culture and how we as women negotiate the challenge of patriarchy.

Ela: In terms of culture, if we look firstly how we understand culture; is it our religion? Is it our customs, which are determined by religion, or the way we dress, and the food we eat? What defines culture? It is a huge topic. It is difficult to say which one we are talking about, what kind of issues Taking it from the point of view of religion for instance then I will talk about the Hindu religion, because I am a Hindu.

Other Indians are Christians, Muslims, etc. so it's not an Indian sort of thing. So if we look at it from the Hindu point of view, then there are a number of customs, and a number of traditions in Hindu religion, like Christianity isn't the same for everybody, you get different differences in the Hindu religion, like you get Christians who are Anglicans and Catholics and Protestants.

In the Hindu religion, you get some who are very very conservative, and some that are very progressive, So between the two there are a whole lot of differences. In traditional Hinduism, there are a number of things women are not allowed to do, they cannot become priests, and there are a number of responsibilities that women have to take in terms of when you give birth, when you are mourning, in terms of women's role in society. In traditional Hinduism, they are very oppressive towards women.

On the other hand, you get Hindu religion which is progress which allows women to have equal rights, it allows women to become priests. There is a lot more powers that women have in terms of the progressive Hindu religion. For me, that is where I come from and that it is what I believe. Men and women are equal. You can also do whatever, there isn't a particular role, and everything is shared responsibility.

That is what my grandfather preached, that is what I believe in, and it is also in terms of other religions, what the progressive Hindu's say, "religion is a personal thing, and because it is personal, you believe in whatever you believe in whatever you want to believe in." *Hinduism allows that. So if you feel closer to any other religion, you think about it. It is so broad, that it doesn't contradict. There is no need for a Christian or a Muslim to convert as such. You can be a good*

Christian, and still be a good Hindu, you can be a good Muslim and still be a good Hindu.

J: I noticed the picture on your wall of the Dala Lama, and Bishop Tutu. Have you met them?

Ela: Yes, yes.

J: How was the meeting?

Ela: I belong to the World Council on Religion and Peace, WCRP, and the International President of the organization, and we invited His Holiness to South Africa. Archbishop Tutu is our Honorary President in our chapter of SA. That is how they met.

J: In this meeting is there anything in particular you remember?

Ela: Both of them have a strong spiritual background; their messages are profound and embrace a wide range of issues that humankind faces today. Everything, like environmental issues they talk about, justice, natural justice, human rights.

J: Natural justice?

Ela: Natural justice is what has been there for years and years, and years which was given to us from the old days, it not because there's a law. Simple things like people are innocent until proven guilty; a person has a right to representation, a right to speak for himself. Those are issues of natural justice.

J: I am most interested in hearing about Albertina Sisulu's funeral that you attended a few days ago. This must have been quite profound for you.

Ela: Yes, it was. Before the funeral, they had a number of memorial services for her in every area. It was well organized, a state funeral. The coffin was draped in the national flag, and took the coffin to the grave. The speeches from the grandchildren and children. What came from the heart, was from the family when they talked about her love. The way she was a natural mother to people. The wonderful person she was. She didn't put herself before anything else. Everybody else came before her. That selflessness, that kindness in her nursing profession.

J: Did you work with her during the Struggle years?

Ela: Yes a lot. We worked many years in Parliament together. I worked with her during the time we established the women's organization in Durban. That is time I met Diana (Russell), just before we started the organization, I was banned at the time.

We had many discussions with her about how we should move forward; she was a great inspiration for us. There were times we would get so disillusioned and feel like we couldn't move, because the Security Police were harassing our members, and so much intimidation at that time, we had to be very very careful about what we did and how we did. At times, it became a burden and you would feel frustrated. Is there any hope in whatever we are doing? Are we going anywhere?

MaSisulu would come and she would just talk to us. Everybody would get enthusiastic. She had that spiriting essence which would rekindle everyone into action. *"Let's do things, we can't just sit back and not do anything."*

J: Aren't you glad you went?

Ela: Yes, it was difficult to decide whether or not to go. It was quite a distance. But I felt I had to do that (Ela wrote about it in her newspaper).

J: Albertina left quite a legacy. You and I both are grandmothers, Ela. In terms of your own legacy, what do you think you want your grandchildren and the children of your grandchildren to remember you for?

Ela: I think the important thing toward the next generation of children is how can we conserve? How can we move away from the high consumerist society that we have become?

How can we really look at **our values**? We didn't think, at that time, how much it would cost to do **this.?**. If there was something we had to do, we had to do it, and people would just put in the money in order to get it done. Even if it was their last cent, they would do it.

But today, the first question is what is it for me? What will I get, when doing something. I think that is becoming more and more prevalent in our society. I would like to see my grandchildren moving away from that kind of selfishness.

J: During the Struggle, there was a common holding together of people. I heard recently, someone say, there was a "suffering point." back in those days.

Ela: It depends, because what is happening now is those people who participated in the Struggle in the past feel that because they participated, they have to have benefits, all the benefits of today. What are they? They are looking at material things in terms of a car, a house. They are not thinking of it from the point of view of the spiritual or the inner aesthetic benefit of living in a society where there are no longer prejudices.

There *are prejudices*, you cannot get around human prejudices, but it's not legalized. There are laws against prejudices, which is the difference from the past to the present. They are not looking at that. They are looking at what materially have I gained, and if I haven't gained then there is **definitely** someone to blame. So all the anger is released upon the government, and to an extent, it's also the governments fault because a lot of people who are in government, not all, but a lot of them are there to build their own empires.

They have also forgotten what they have fought for.

J: I remember reading a thought from Bishop Tutu, "My greatest fear is when the oppressed become the oppressor."

I see on your bookshelf, President Obama's book "Dreams of my Father". I was wondering if your name comes from your father or your mother?

Ela: My father is Gandhi's son.

J: The world still remembers your grandfather. It's amazing, nobody forgets his name. People might forget a number of our US presidents. But not the name Mandela. There certainly is a spirit here in South Africa that can bring out the best in human behavior.

Ela: The Gandhi legacy.

J: Yes.

Ela: The Gandhi legacy was strong during the Struggle years, because everybody spoke about what Gandhi had taught how to be moved in the non violent legacy, because even though the ANC had taken to heart, but it wasn't all the ANC members, there was a societal group of people in the country who wanted to peaceful resolution to the whole problem; and how we can non violently struggle for our rights.

The most democratic struggle in the country was based on non-violent strategies, and the anti apartheid movement was based on non-violent strategies.

J: As we move forward, I wonder if there is any possible way to work.. all work together in a peaceful way. We hear about my government and other governments stepping into assist in building democratic societies, (in the Middle Eastern countries). It's such a concern, I wonder if we will ever return to those non-violent peaceful ways to protest.

Ela: Umm. I think there is a move to work for non-violent peaceful ways. If we see the last few months of unrest in Northern Africa, you see that most of them opted for non-violent means in Egypt and most of the countries. So people are beginning to look at non-violent solutions even in Pakistan. It's not being published, our press feels it needs to publish things that sell and when they publish all the killings, they think it sells better

When a person is marching peacefully, nobody is interested in that. "What bleeds leads" they come from that kind of mentality. That's the lead story.

Actually, there is a group in the States has produced a CD, "From the Power of Non-Violence". They actually went out and filmed the countries that had peaceful changed.

J: It sounds like you are still very hopeful.

Ela: I *am hopeful. Because I think now, hope, is the only thing left.* What else can we do? If we have wars, it will destroy the world.

J: This is certainly true. Can you share a little about your grandfather?

Ela: Often when I remember him, I think of him sitting quietly and spinning at wooden wheel. He felt 'spinning' was part of economic change; it gave a livelihood to every person and brought people together.

J: I tried to spin, it is not easy. Your grandfather is my hero.

Ela: He was a hero for me as well, as he is a hero for everyone else. Being the granddaughter does bring one close to him, but that is not the reason he is my hero. His teachings and his life has inspired me and a million others.

Ela Gandhi and Elizabeth Franklin, friend of Jeannine's and native of South Africa - 2011

Going Home

Home to Portland
1991

Zamora's gift of his last diamond was my only true treasure as I put my American life back together and made a new home for myself.

At the time, I had no possible idea how Zamora's diamond could bring me back to Africa. I was content enough when I remembered his words, "Clarity cannot be seen by the naked eye". What I needed now, was to be my bravest and enter back into my own culture.

Leaving Africa proved far more wrenching than I'd ever imagined. I had embraced the stories that unfolded, and the monumental changes of a New South Africa. I witnessed a country whose hero was also their beloved president, Nelson Mandela.

Several years passed, a new dream was coming into focus. It would keep what I had learned in Africa alive. Someday, some way I wanted to take high school students to work and discover how Africa doesn't need them, they need Africa. As the dream grew, I could see ways to create unique experiences in rural villages. Perhaps in time this would be my legacy, and as it was given to me it would be mine to give away.

Africa taught me by the simple practice of their humanity. It had transformed me by forging a confidence and resolve I had never felt until leaving my comfort zone.

The dream had to be set aside for a time. My belief system was changing from the inside out. Leopard instincts had followed me home. Work was satisfying, my social life not so much. Portland was a great city, leaving Eugene was a good idea. There was nothing in my hometown but old memories and pieces of myself left along the way. I wanted to believe I was strong enough to "delve into places that needed healing."

A journey began, with the challenge of a new belief system, to love and be loved. First, I thought I must believe there were *a few good men out there*. That was a long bridge to cross, but a necessary passage. Three years later, I was introduced to Mark Smith. The only problem was that he was happily living back in my home town. Love entered the picture, and I began working hard thinking about returning to Eugene.

A marriage proposal came December 29 1995. Zamora's diamond gift was cut in half and hand carved into our gold wedding bands. Mark and I were married in June of 1996 and began our new lives together in Eugene.

Many nights were spent reminiscing about long forgotten dreams. Mark asked about what was important for me. "Returning to Africa" was my quick reply. I shared with him how Zamora said the diamond would have the power to bring me back.

And it has.

Small Village Foundation

The Journey

The Small Village Foundation (SVF) is a non-profit humanitarian organization dedicated to and to providing opportunities for Idahoans to use their talents to help others and, in the process, improving the lives of rural Africans.

Based in Boise, Idaho, the Small Village Foundation accomplishes these goals by funding a variety of clean water, education, and health projects in rural African villages and by providing opportunities for American high school students and adults to travel to rural African villages to engage in hands-on humanitarian projects. Small Village Foundation humanitarian projects and trips changes the lives — and hearts — of all those who participate in them.

AIDS is ravaging Africa and as a result often kills both parents and, leaves school-aged children as head of households. In many cases, these children must quit school to care for younger siblings.

In 2005, SVF established a crèche, day nursery, in Centocow, South Africa. Using a building that has been donated, SVF has provided funding to hire teachers, a cook and to purchase food for up to 70 children every school day.

In addition to funding the crèche, SVF has completed other projects to enhance education including sending a 1,000 pounds of text and library books, and provided computers for a high school. SVF has also built playgrounds and a library and provided clean water throughout rural villages.

Most recently, the old donated building was torn down and replaced it with a new structure as seen below. The school has fulfilled the necessary criteria for the South African government to do the funding.

Photos from the Journey

Ghana West Africa
2003

Idaho Students to Africa
2005-2006

Zulu shield presented to Mayor David Bieter of Boise, Idaho

Voices from the Travelers

Dee Bowling
SVF Board Member

"On an empty stomach?

Memorize a foreign language in a classroom in 100-degree heat?

Bamboi, Ghana in West Africa has a primary school, junior secondary school, and a small Catholic school, where many children go to school *hungry each day.*

The classrooms are bare with only a large chalkboard for *the day's lesson to be memorized.* Students sit attentively knowing they are the fortunate ones to be in school."

Dana Capps

As an undergraduate I studied Economics and International Affairs at the University of Mary Washington. I feel my draw to those fields of study were subconsciously ignited by my Ghanaian experience, seeing sprawling cities, such as Accra, characterized by wonton infrastructure, and small villages, such as Bamboi, nestled into rural scenery of extreme poverty. After college I sought out other cultural experiences, namely teaching English in South Korea for nearly three years. I loved teaching and working with children, and continued that as a cross country/track coach upon moving back to Boise.

Currently, I'm about to start graduate school at the University of California Berkeley to obtain a master's degree in architecture—a culturally embedded, yet literal framework for living standards. I think my brief time in Bamboi really touched the piece of me that appreciates the magic amalgamation of landscape, building, and personality. In Bamboi it was easy to see that the mud structures were just as much a reflection of the red and yellow landscape, as the people were a reflection of their intimate community. The people of Bamboi comprised a *small village* where relationships, kindness, generosity, and gratitude trumped a dire lack of material and money—a way of life I try to channel every day.

Kira Thorien

"Our group poured every ounce of heart and fiber into this expedition. The images of green mambas, scorpions, and malaria have now faded. I am reminded of the innocent pure friendship of the Ghanaian people."

Ty Waters

Ty learning to thatch a roof

UPON LEAVING GHANA IN 2003: "Leaving was the hardest part. When the van door shut, I wanted to stay. I wanted to take the feeling of the village home with me, knowing I needed nothing to be happy."

IN 2013 AS TY PREPARES TO BEGIN MEDICAL SCHOOL: "After graduating from Capital High School I went to University of Idaho and got a degree in sports science and exercise physiology. I then finished a few more courses at Boise State (although I am still a diehard Vandal) and applied for medical school. I was accepted this year to University of Nevada School of Medicine and will start class in August. Our trip to Bamboi was actually what I consider the experience that influenced me to pursue a career in medicine (I even wrote about it in my personal statement when applying to medical school). It was on that trip that I decided I wanted a career where my purpose was to help others, and the most literal way I could help others. I found being a physician was a way to help others on a very fundamental level: with their health. From that point on, I began working toward getting into medical school.

Aside from just doing school stuff, I went to Uganda to work in an emergency room in 2011 and also got married and now have two children, Alivia (4 years old) and Marcus (4 months old). Every day, I hope that they have a similarly rewarding experience as that which I was fortunate enough to have by being involved with Small Village Foundation."

Basanti Bail

"In a room at the (Valley of a Thousand Hills) clinic, a small boy came in and sat down. Dr. Mark, (a dentist from Boise, Idaho) asked him if he had any pain and if so where. With huge eyes like an ocean and with his heart and soul riding the waves, he pointed to where the pain was and said, "it really hurts."

With a small voice, but full of courage he said, "I won't cry." We had to ask him if anyone could consent to his operation because of liability issues. "Any family close by none...grandparents... none. anyone who could sign...none."

"I won't cry" was ringing in my ears. "Please," he said, "Give me the tools I will do it myself." My heart broke and right then and there I wanted to do something, anything to take away his pain. He walked so far to receive this rejection. He kept his pain. As he walked out the door, and out of my life forever, I saw his eyes, they were now like the sand, lifeless."

Taylor Barnwell

"Upon our arrival a group of small children stood and faced us and started singing. When they finished there was a silent awkward pause. We just stood there. A young 5-year-old boy came, grabbed my hand and led us out to a field to play.

The children didn't see differences between us. We were all people.

While staying in Soweto, we slept on the cold ground and bathed by washing in a rusted bucket of chilled water. We listened to their stories of the 'hard times during the apartheid years'.

One night, I walked alone through the cold darkness of a dirty alley. I passed houses and expected glares and dirty looks. I was terrified of running into someone. I was scared of what could happen, especially after all the persecutions the black South Africans endured.

But, as I looked up, people smiled and waved at me. Some of the neighbors came into the street and greeted me. I was astonished at how friendly and outgoing they were. They actually cared about me. These people were so happy and owned practically nothing. These amazing people showed me how I wanted to live my life."

Corynn Hower

"Being African American in Boise, Idaho, and adopted is not always easy. I found out so much about myself. I found roots that made me feel completely rooted to the earth. They are still growing. I have to keep watering my roots every day.

I learned I can go any place in the world and still be okay. I will do just fine. I can help and be helped.

In Africa, I found home."

Dani Long

"In our final home stay in Soweto, we were deemed South African names -Nokusa, pronounced No-guu-saa, meaning "mother of dawn." It was derived from my passion for stars and the effect my smile has on the breaking of day. Words are powerful.

I recall the lurching of my stomach at the mention of the words shots and snakes. I realized that all the hours I had put into dreading this trip had been redeemed through the pronunciation of six letters. Those letters, held dear to me now, as I proudly pronounce them in a foreign tongue. They stand for the voyage to South Africa; which gives light to the power of wisdom and the awakening of knowledge."

Anneliese Rice

"In my life, experiences with compassionate people have changed my direction and perspective. I recently visited South Africa with a small group of students and adults.

The poverty there would have been overwhelming if the people we encountered had been less happy and warm. For example, we visited and worked at an orphanage for several days where nearly all the kids had lost family member to AIDS.

Everyone had been through tragedy beyond my experience. Yet, without hesitation, they embraced our group. They wanted to be affectionate and friendly with us all the time. They knew we were staying for a short time, but they still invested in us emotionally.

For me to love them in return was automatic. Saying goodbye was harrowing, but the experience worth more than my sorrow."

Shanelle Galloway

Utah State University

English-Creative Writing/Organizational Communications

"Going to South Africa increased my appreciation for just about everything I have, especially the opportunity to obtain my education. One day, I want be part of a non-profit organization. I have never forgotten my journey to Africa. I often asked myself how could these loving forgiving people be so happy in their difficult circumstances. It is if all the love makes up for all they don't have.

Being African American myself, I was constantly explaining, "No, I don't know Will Smith."

I am more confident in myself. I know I can make it through anything, and that I can be happy no matter what situation. It has been almost 5 years since my trip; it is my dream to return, perhaps to Ghana to teach English in an orphanage.

For all its good and bad, you can't help falling in love with it; astonished at how friendly and outgoing they were. They actually cared about me.

These people were so happy and owned practically nothing. These amazing people showed me how I wanted to live my life."

Kate O'Neill

"My time in South Africa while short was filled with many lessons that I have taken to heart. But with one word I can sum up all the lessons that still connect me to Africa today, smile. No matter where we were or whom we were with, there was a smile to be seen. Smiles from the women who worked at Bobby Bear, smiling even through the horror that they had witnessed. Smiles from the children at the schools we visited. They were the most sincere smiles I had ever seen coming from people that had more than multiple reasons to frown. These smiles taught me to look for the good in any situation, to search for the good that can be found within every person and to smile no matter what curve life may throw at me."

Patty O'Neill

(Kate O'Neill's mother)

"There is nothing like returning to a place that remains unchanged to find the ways in which you yourself have altered." – Nelson Mandela

My father asked me why in the world I would let my 16-year-old daughter venture half way around the globe to the farthest ends of Africa, a place no one in my family had ever traveled to. It was a question I was really not prepared to fully answer until Katie, my oldest of two children had gone and then returned safely from a 2009 trip with Small Village to South Africa.

Originally, I was hoping to open a window unto the world for my daughter. To show her that our world was not just a little town in a remote state in one country but rather it was a huge and hopefully inviting gift just waiting to be explored and valued beyond measure. I wanted to instill in her that we are so privileged to live in this part of the world and there are many places where others aren't as fortunate. I was hoping the trip itself would be the lesson.

The trip was a great teaching tool but it was also much more than that. Small Village's student journeys founded by Jeannine Antoniou Smith ended up being a life alteration. Katie and subsequently my son Patrick, who just returned the 2013 Small Village Foundation's South Africa trip, were both changed forever. They went out into the big wide world, discovered South Africa, the beautiful culture and people, then returned home to Boise, a "place that remained unchanged" and found that it was they themselves who were forever altered. Their appreciation for all that we have: clean water, a sturdy roof over their heads, food at the ready, clothing to choose from … things we all take for granted, were in their newfound reality, really blessings to be cherished."

Katherine

Photo by John Slattery

"The majority of my time spent in Africa was truly moving. However, one specific event that sticks in my mind happened the first day we worked in Centocow on Vulinqondo crèche. After a long morning of painting and plastering, we were rewarded with our well-deserved lunch. Before we even started work on the crèche in the morning, I noticed a few small children playing with a rag ball a few yards down the dirt road.

I asked the chaperones if I could give the kids one of our soccer balls, but they told me that bringing the shiny new balls out would start a frenzy and no work would be done. This broke my heart, so while everyone was preoccupied with their sandwiches, Lily Zimmer and I took one of the balls and snuck away to the kids yard.

All of the very small kids scurried away, but the older one (somewhere near 7 years old) stayed. Because of the language barrier I could do nothing but gesture and hold the ball out to the child. He desperately wanted the ball so he rushed out to us, carefully took it from my outreached hands, admired it for a moment, looked at us with a wide smile and grateful eyes and embraced us. He then ran back to his hut screaming and skipping, holding his new ball high in the air for everyone to see. Dumbfounded by this reaction Lily and I just stood there and stared. We heard from past trips that soccer balls were the equivalent to gold, but we weren't quite sure what to expect. This small act of generosity was just a taste of what was to come, but it was definitely a sweet one!"

Reflections

By Dr Mark Smith

Looking east out the window of the one room dental clinic, the hills roll before me like waves in the ocean. The dental clinic had not been used in five years.

Like some kind of squatter, I unloaded two suitcases of dental supplies and equipment. The word went out 'the dentist is here' and soon a line of people with anxious faces formed a line by the door.

Most had never seen a dentist. Tolerating toothaches is a part of life in a rural village.

Afterthoughts

As today's *hunters-gathers*, we search beyond mapped borders and find unexpected meaning. We hesitate in the reflection of our own Apartheid, a self-separation, confining ourselves and limiting our understanding of those who do not look like us.

We are captivated by the unexplained. At times, we explore a clairsentient knowing in the ancient African tradition of THROWING THE BONES.

Are not our children and grandchildren to be the hunters-gatherers of their own lives?

They expect beauty and experience pain, 'breaking the shell of understanding'. They leave with curiosity, hesitation and return connected to their humanity. They go with questions and come back content with questions unanswered. They see rawness, at times a searing rawness exposing life in most of the world.

They try to explain life's extremes. They try.

"They are the sons and daughters of Life's longing for itself," penned the Lebanese poet, Kahlil Gibran.

Are we not all hunters-gatherers, to rise above our shadow side, like the leopard, to 'keep hoping when there is little hope.'

About the Author

Jeannine Antoniou Smith grew up in Eugene, Oregon. After she studied at Brigham Young University, she returned to raise her family in Eugene. Always intrigued in the world around her, and the many lands abroad, she founded a sister city for Eugene with Kagegawa, Japan, and a sister city for Boise, Idaho with Jiacheng, China.

She has lived in Taipei, Taiwan in The Republic of China and Swaziland, South Africa.

Jeannine was a committee member of CASI Foundation for Children – China 2001 where she helped to establish a home-like orphanage. Also, she is the founder of the Small Village Foundation – 2002.

Jeannine lives in Boise, Idaho with her husband, Dr. Mark E. Smith. She can be reached at jeanninesmith@aol.com.

CPSIA information can be obtained at www.ICGtesting.com
Printed in the USA
LVOW12s1944161113

361592LV00003B/665/P